With the

Bob Able

24/2/2024

Third Helpings of Spain Tomorrow

Bob Able

For all of us who have been through so much.

THIRD HELPINGS OF SPAIN TOMORROW

By Bob Able

The third book in Bob Able's Bestselling 'Spain Tomorrow' memoir series

Cover Image: Original painting by Clare Burnett. Clare Burnett is a talented artist who is available to take commissions and creates exclusive paintings, line drawings and artwork. She can produce wall art, placemats, special occasion cards, stationary and book covers.
Contact her at: **clarepaints4u@yahoo.com**

With special thanks to Philip Wood for his help with proofreading, editing and his encouragement.

CHAPTER 1

'**S**low You Down' the occasional humorous signs beside the roads in Rural and Coastal North Norfolk advise, and they have a point. Quite apart from the obvious caution to motorists to respect the quiet roads of this sleepy county, there is a message for us all about the pace of life, which we ignore at our peril.

But such a lot has happened so fast in the world since 2020 when I last put finger to keyboard in this chronicle, and so much of it was unreservedly bad, that to go over it all again would make grim reading. Since my object in these scratchings is to amuse and entertain, I can assure you, gentle reader, that although we must touch on that dreadful period for historical context, we are not going to be looking over our shoulder in too much detail. We will merely glance into the abyss of the Covid Horror and the Political Pandemonium of that period as we speed by … And Brexit? … well, least said soonest mended!

Can I, instead, thank and congratulate you if you have

read Spain Tomorrow and More Spain Tomorrow, and remind you where we left matters at the end of the last instalment.

I was, you will recall, really quite unwell and suffering at the hands of my medical advisers with the effects of hormone therapy as I waited, and waited, for my cancer treatments to begin.

Now I've been yanked back from the cliff edge. The treatment, for now at least, is complete. I can report that all is well and I am still, for the most part, functioning! Not cured, but at least moving forward.

I'll take a moment here to thank most sincerely all the many readers who reached out and got in touch to wish me well during that darkest of periods. Your kind thoughts and good wishes carried me through it all and I am most grateful to you.

I have to say I was also very surprised at how many readers had noticed my plight. You don't make very much money at all out of writing books so, looking at the tiny income levels, I had thought I might have sold a couple of dozen books, but it seems the numbers ran much higher than that, and I was truly blown away by how many people cared.

So, shall we catch up on what has been happening since we last touched base?

The slightly crazy world of Bob and Bee does not stand still, no matter what obstacles we have to surmount, and Bee had been bustling about with her usual determination to keep us focussed on having fun. But there was no getting away from it, Covid-19 changed everything.

When 'Social Distancing' became the norm and holidays no longer involved carefree jet flights to crowded beaches, we all tried hard to keep away from each other, while longing to be together.

But you can't keep Bob and Bee down for long, so in this memoir I'll tell you what we did about it, and how we tried to ensure we could travel safely (lockdowns allowing) and holiday at home and abroad while the 'pandemic' raged.

It's certainly not all doom and gloom though, and we had some very amusing moments.

We still yearned to keep travelling, so we bought a secondhand motorhome. Our own little Covid-safe bubble, we thought. But we knew nothing about motorhomes, and we hadn't been near a camp site for over twenty years, so we would have to learn from scratch.

Covid caused delays with the delivery of the motorhome too. Having moved the due date back once already, the dealer again complained that they may not have time to fit the expensive habitation air conditioning (essential for Spain) and the refillable gas system, which we had ordered to be fitted in time for the agreed collection date.

We could not move that date because of my pending

treatment, and after some heated discussions, where it became clear that the sales people had over-promised and the workshops could not deliver, a compromise was reached.

The complicated re-fillable gas system would now be fitted by others at a later date and the cost deducted from the bill, but the vehicle would be ready for collection, with all the rest of the work done, on the agreed day.

Fortunately, when at last it was ready, there was one point in our favour in that the quotation we got to fit the gas system from another dealer much closer to our home was some £300 cheaper than the original dealer's price. It was nice to win one back for a change, and Bee announced that she would like a folding bicycle to take with us on our travels, so the saving funded that.

The motorhome, after its initial drive home from the supplying dealer, had to sit on our drive for now though, as the first set of my radiotherapy treatments was about to start.

But when we did get to use it I kept notes, of course, so let's see how we coped on our first proper trip in the motorhome …

… I was jerked from a dreamless sleep by a vicious burst of drumming.

It had been like this, on and off, pretty much since teatime, and whilst there was no sign of any ingress of water through the motorhome roof, it was certainly being tested throughly.

In Spain, where we intended to take our new motorhome when we got used to it, they call this sort of downpour a 'Gota Fria' and whilst common enough there, it was an unusual and disturbing experience where we were parked, on a patch of grass, in a deserted English orchard. But, even if further sleep was impossible, at least we had escaped from the confines of the house, if only for a little while.

'I think we had better get up and move the van, Bee,' I said, as a groan confirmed that she too was not asleep.

It was too dark to see anything through the windows, but I envisaged the broad grassed area outside was either several inches deep in water, or a muddy quagmire from which it might be difficult to extract our not quite new but still eye-wateringly expensive motorhome.

It turned out to be neither flood nor quagmire, and for now the field was still soaking up the rain, more or less. But it was a close run thing, and just as well we moved when we did.

We were very new to 'motor-homing', and this visit to an apple orchard in rural Suffolk was only the second venture we had dared to take in ours. Unable to get to Spain, we were now part of the new Covid-19 driven boom in motorhome ownership, seeking our own 'bubble' to be able to get out and about, in the UK at least, in relative safety, as the virus curtailed our wider travel plans.

However, by the middle of the week, we were really just sitting ducks in a massive rainstorm which continued relentlessly until we made a break for home. Those ducks may have enjoyed the weather, but as 'newbie motor-homers', it made us very nervous.

As those of you familiar with motorhomes and camper-vans will know, the thinly insulated roofs of even the most expensive vehicles amplify the sound of the weather outside dramatically, and further sleep was impossible.

The setting, however, was delightful, and once we had mastered driving along the narrow lanes approaching it, following the instructions of our new Caravan Club on-line shop sourced Sat.Nav., the first couple of days of our four day trip were warm. Sunny enough to enable us to try out our new folding barbecue and burn some meat.
We even got to unwrap and try our new deckchairs, chosen specifically to fit in the storage hatch on the side of our vehicle without too much of a fight.

The apple harvest was just coming to an end as we arrived in bright sunshine. Our inexperience showing, we made a mess of pitching on the grass field, watched by two other neighbours with touring caravans, who had the only concrete hard standings.
They were being paid to pick the apples, and left soon after our arrival. Something we said? Or did they know something we didn't?

We had found out that the 'set up costs' of acquiring a 'new' motorhome are not limited to a bit of wire to plug in the electricity and some of that special dissolving loo paper they all seem to use. Nothing had come with it so we had to buy all sorts of things for cooking, eating and washing, much as you would to equip a modest flat. It was not a cheap exercise.

Whilst you could buy freshly bottled apple juice and apples at the gate, there were no shops, pubs, or anything much else in walking distance of the site. But there was a little, quite modern, 'garden sauna style' shower room and toilet, which had hot, nay sometimes scalding, water but no heating. There was also a chemical waste dump, quite close to our 'pitch', for emptying the happy camper's toilets which, unfortunately, we had to witness being pumped out on our second day.

Although the apple picking retirees stay put for some time as I understand it, they must make their own amusements. But we, as privileged paying guests rather than workers, could at least watch the owner's jolly little red 1940s tractor puttering through the peaceful orchards collecting the picking boxes, just as it had always done since it arrived brand new on the farm, which was an entertainment in itself.

The flash, drop down TV, in our motorhome worked and was a Godsend in the rain, but before the weather broke we enjoyed delightful walks on the public footpaths which cross the site. With no need to step on a road, we saw green woodpeckers, a buzzard and abundant flora and fauna. Bee also cycled into the excruciatingly pretty village of Debenham, about a mile and a half away, which has a butcher, a co-op and some shops, pubs and tea rooms (all of which were inevitably closed due to the Covid crisis).

Our visit, in late September, would have been ideal if not for the weather, but we had still learned much more about how to set up and cope with our new motorhome. From that point of view it was well worth the £15 a night pitch fee and, when Henry, the charming owner and proprietor of the apple farm, turned up with printed details of the local attractions and an attractive and skilfully hand drawn map of our surroundings, we were made to feel very welcome.

It may not have been Spain, but at least we had escaped and were having a holiday, of sorts, at last.

-ooo0oo-

Lockdown can be tough, but 'shielding', where you are effectively imprisoned with no social contact within your own four walls, can be brutal.

I had to add repeatedly cancelled cancer treatments into the mix, with the fear and desperation which characterised the early months of 2020 as the coronavirus swept, seemingly unchecked, across the world. Until this point my own horizons were reduced to little more than the view from my study window.

You might think conditions would not be ideal for

writing a travel memoir.

Almost as certainly as being placed under house arrest, the chances of escape before we bought our motorhome during the early part of that period were vanishingly small. But when I realised that I had nothing to do … because there was nothing I could do, at least I had time to think.

If you read the first two parts of this memoir series you will know that I have shared my experiences in the less touristy parts of the Costa Blanca and explained how a modest inheritance allowed my long suffering wife Bee and I to buy a holiday home in Spain. But we weren't locked down in Spain, we were in rainy old England when the virus hit … and I was just about to start a lengthy period of cancer treatment which, almost as soon as Covid-19 acquired a familiar name, got cancelled.

When I last wrote about this, in early 2020, in 'More Spain Tomorrow', I was expecting my cancer treatment to start a couple of months later, in March, and was about to undergo a procedure to insert a 'SpaceOAR' device to protect my organs ('Organs At Risk') from the treatment to come. This device has a three month useful life, before it dissolves and is absorbed into the body, so they had to get the treatment done by March.

It had taken since January 2019, when I was initially told I had a problem, to reach this point.

Then, of course, the pandemic erupted and

everything changed overnight.

My treatment got re-scheduled time and again, and it was not until September 2020 that it actually started at long, long last.

This time, if the NHS could not find time and space to treat me, I was informed, I would have to go 'private'; there was now no choice.

Inevitably the 'SpaceOAR' device had long since ceased to function by then, but although it was more risky without it, my treatment simply could not wait any longer. The race was on to beat the spreading cancer; and hopefully Covid wouldn't get me in the meantime.

Against this dull and slightly terrifying background, it is worth recounting what we had hoped 2020 would bring for us before the cup was dashed from our lips, and what we, as 'ordinary people' facing the 'new normal' (ghastly expression), had decided to do about it.

We had planned, and had to cancel, a 'once in a lifetime' safari trip to celebrate Bee's retirement; We had looked into becoming Spanish residents, but Brexit snookered that one. We planned sightseeing trips around Europe, and we had considered buying a very modest villa with a pool, if we could sell our apartment.

None of that happened of course.

But, as I said, you can't keep Bob and Bee down for

long, and despite cancer, Covid, Brexit and one thing and another, I for one absolutely refuse to put a blanket over my head while clutching a mug of soup and just wait to ... and just wait...

So I decided to move things on and in a brief break just before all the lockdowns started, we snatched a short trip to Spain.

CHAPTER 2

'Asociación Protectora Amigos del Caballo,' or more usually just APAC, is a tiny but remarkable charity, run to rescue abused or abandoned horses, with a couple of fields, a ramshackle building or two, and a dedicated and determined group of people from various countries who work hard to offer care to their charges.

We first heard about the charity when we were invited to sample what was described as 'an enormous gin and tonic' in a little cortijo down in the campo at the bottom of 'our' mountain.

Every Sunday morning a little ritual is performed by those in the know. The narrow country road is filled with a motley collection of vehicles trying to squeeze into the sections where the lane is just slightly wider, along the mostly single track road, and park without blocking the roadway completely. It is a good job that this part of the exercise takes place before the gin is poured!

Somehow these visitors manage to get out of their parking slots later, when the gin has been drunk, but perhaps we had better not go into that too deeply.

I have formed a firm friendship with one of the 'regulars' who moderately sensibly leaves his car at home on these occasions, and describes the makeshift bar and the facilities within as 'the dirtiest bar on earth, but also one of the warmest and most welcoming'. The work they do, depending entirely on donations and generous contributions made in return for the gin and other drinks (this is not an 'official' bar) liberally dispensed by Lois, the charming and chatty hostess who runs the charity, is quite amazing. Eschewing the difficulties of the parking arrangements, my friend turns up most Sundays on a moped, and as far as I know, rides it home as well!

The Sunday morning bar was a masterstroke in getting people to support the charity, and APAC struggled through Covid just managing to keep the horses fed as a result. They kept going by imposing 'social distancing' for visitors and saying they must keep 'one pony apart', and did their best to keep trying to improve their charges health and basic needs throughout the pandemic.

Some of the stories of how the horses came to be here are sad, and some are bound to raise the spirits, as does the gin, and warm the hearts of those who meet them.

Take for example a middle aged horse named 'Lord', who is completely blind. When APAC rescued him and his companion, a pony named 'Lucio', they were alone in the world and probably about to become cat food. But once they got to APAC and were released into the yard, Lucio, with a series of nudges, steered Lord around the facilities, kept him out of danger and was always at his side. The two were inseparable and soon had a following of volunteers who were charmed by their antics.

APAC's activities are not just restricted to horses either, they have taken in goats, dogs and donkeys, and a couple of cats seem to have adopted them and keep the rodent population under control around the feed rooms.

Fancy a look around the 'dirtiest bar on earth'? Oh, I think we should ...

Having dealt with the car parking, one approaches a tall metal gate behind a small concreted area usually occupied by the owner's grimy and battered 'people carrier', used to shift straw and horse feed as much as people these days. Through the gate, on a strip of concrete enclosed by makeshift fences, we come to another gate, and once through that, we find ourselves in a scruffy yard.

To one side there is an area of uneven currently wet concrete with a dribbling hose, a couple of elderly wheelbarrows, a broom and a dusty motorbike with only one wheel. To the right, in front of the first of the collection of untidy buildings is a rusty pick-up truck with its bonnet up, and to the left the little path, now just beaten earth, leads us on towards our goal.

Over a series of once white low concrete walls with occasional piers supporting stout timber poles, and steering our way around stacks of those black rubber buckets so beloved of Spanish workmen (some full and steaming), we can see some horses corralled in a yard. There is a huge 'muck-pile', more brooms and various rusty agricultural implements, and another collection of little low roofed storage buildings. Then the quiet scene is split asunder by the barking of a huge dog, contained in a rickety low building that looks as though it might collapse at any moment. But we notice, thankfully, that the dog is attached to a stout rope.

This little building marks the beginning of the reason we have come here … 'the bar'.

Initially things get a bit more familiar. There are a couple of mis-matched bar tables and chairs with umbrellas, and although the ground beneath our feet is uneven and just soil with weeds breaking through the well trampled surface here and there, there are smiling people with glasses in their hands.

A few steps further brings us under a shaded area, with the hot sun blocked and diffused by a collection of tired woven fence panels and canvas sheets laid over the roofing beams, and there before us at last is the bar!

Closer examination reveals that the bar itself is constructed from a couple of doors, some pallets and what looks like a once ornate wardrobe on its side!

No matter, there is the smiling Lois and she has a gin bottle in her hand … let the revels commence!

The bar area is not 'dirty' because it is ill-kept or unhygienic, but if you have ever had anything to do with stables you will know that trying to keep the area clean is an impossibility. The constant dust, hay, straw and people tramping about in boots sees to that.

A small pack of dogs approaches us now, some exuberantly welcoming, some holding back shyly, and they are dismissed by a word from Lois. We notice the eclectic collection of barstools on the trampled soil and places to perch drinks, seemingly made from whatever fell to hand.

Jack and Daniel a pair of young German Shepherds, who were handed over by a naive former owner who didn't offer them any training and then complained that they were unmanageable, came to greet us next. Now beautifully behaved thanks to the intervention of the charity's various volunteers they gently say 'hello' and then retreat to positions under the bar tables and lie down on the earth.

Time to order drinks.

Well, it is certainly not 'the dirtiest bar on earth'

judging by the glasses and scrupulous hygiene practices behind the bar. There might not be a polished tile floor or waiters and waitresses in smart uniforms, but there is nothing wrong with how the drinks are dispensed. Gleaming huge fishbowl-like glasses are produced. Drawn, presumably from an unseen dishwasher outback, just out of sight, … an ice making machine must live in there as well it would seem … and juniper berries are sprinkled liberally as the gin is poured, or should that be sloshed, into the glasses.

No British optics or mean little measures here. Just up-end the bottle and splash it in! Tonic? Say when.
Phew! Those gins have AUTHORITY!

We squeezed onto a couple of elderly barstools by the grimy white wall separating us from the stable yard and learned something of the often sad history of how each of the horses came to be here. When either Jack or Daniel, I'm not sure which, came and sat leaning on my stool I had to turn and sit with my back to the horses if I didn't want to rest my feet on the poor dogs back, which seemed a little rude as we had only just been introduced.

Horses are inquisitive creatures and it was not long before they started to approach the dividing wall to see who these new people were, and to enquire whether we had anything for them?

Fortunately, Bee had bought along some carrots, which made us very popular guests indeed.

But the carrots were soon gone, and most of the horses sidled off to see if any of the other customers had anything for them. All, that is, except one particularly large animal who stood just behind me with his head over the wall waiting expectantly, just in case.

Time passed. The level of the gin went down. The conversation became more exuberant as we were introduced to more of the customers and supporters of the charity as they passed by on their way to the bar. They came from all over Europe and it was interesting to hear their stories. Several of the volunteers brought plates of homemade tapas to hand round, or just crisps and nuts.

All of the customers circulated, but not the horse who seemed to be a permanent fixture just behind me.

Then, during a pause in the ebb and flow of customers going to the bar he suddenly took a half step back and sneezed with such violence that I received approximately half a pint of glutinous horse snot right between the shoulder blades, on my new shirt!

Paper towels were found. The laughter eventually died down and, gin finished, we tottered to the car and home, with me trying not to sit back in the seat, so that my much abused shirt did not make contact with the upholstery!

We were invited back again the following week, but elected to sit a little closer to the bar and away from the wall where the horses lived this time!

Tragically I have learned that the blind horse's companion, Lucio, died recently, so Lord is without his guide. The volunteers have made arrangements to feed him separately so that he is not bullied away from the feed and I can report that, now that he knows his way around, although he obviously will be missing his companion, he is happy enough.

He has been joined by another recently rescued horse with severe cataracts. Maybe they will help each other out.

He may team up with one of the other horses who has learned how to unlock the bolt on the feed store and open the gate, if one of the willing helpers forgets to put the padlock on it!

I thought you might be interested, so details of the APAC charity and how to help the horses and all the other animals at the facility appear at the end of this book. The bar may be dirty, but it is built with love and compassion by those who care for the animals nobody else wants.

-ooOOoo-

Back home, as the lockdowns started, I knew before it arrived that I was going to get the 'shielding' letter from the UK Government , following conversations with my doctor.

I found out that I had been admitted to the 'extremely vulnerable' club and qualified, due to the cancer and my lifelong asthma, as one of those considered most 'at risk', should I come into contact with this nasty virulent upper respiratory tract infection.

I knew I was a sitting duck.

My youngest son, David, who lived at home with us at the time, continued to work because his employer deemed him an essential worker, and as he came and went each day we realised we had to be extremely careful.

'This letter says you should stay in one room and keep out of shared areas,' announced Bee. 'Do you want me to make up a bed in your study?'

I did not, and I said so. We would be scrupulous about hygiene and social contact, but I was not going to be imprisoned in one room, thank you very much.

'What would they have me do,' I asked, 'live on pizza?'

'What are you talking about? Who said anything about pizza?' Bee looked quizzical.

'Well, it's the only thing you will be able to slide under the door,' I quipped.

'Pizza is fattening,' said Bee firmly. So that was that off the menu.

In Spain, our delightful apartment, on a mountain, with views across the golf course to the Mediterranean beyond, sat alone, but certainly not unloved.

It was not really empty either. I had spent our last few visits equipping it with various items from my wardrobe, along with medicines, toiletries and creature comforts, including a full wine rack. My idea was partly to ensure we only needed hand luggage when we grabbed cheap flights, but also so that we were instantly 'at home' as soon as we opened the door.

'Daft,' said Bee, when we had an unseasonably sunny spring in England and I realised that all my short sleeved shirts and shorts were gathering dust in Spain.

The sun was nice, but I noticed something odd.

The sun in Spain, or at least in our bit of it, is different. Here, in rural Norfolk, when I could go outside as we moved the deckchairs round the garden to catch the last rays, it was not the same.
Perhaps it was the humidity, or maybe the pollution, but a sunny day in England does lack that feeling of wellbeing I had experienced in Spain.
Possibly it was just the sense of being 'on holiday' we were missing, as the UK Government produced all sorts of stuff about 'protecting our mental health' under lockdown to 'help'.

I didn't think I had a mental health problem until the Government drew the possibility to my attention, but their suggestions succeeded in giving me one more thing to worry about. Until, that is, I made a decision.

'Blow this, Bee,' I said, 'I might be locked in, but I refuse to be down as well! I'm going to do something about it!'

So I did.

You may laugh, but I decided to become a best selling author.

CHAPTER 3

Thanks to Brexit as much as the virus, the British economy had tanked, and our political leaders continued to shoot themselves in the foot in their attempts to rescue the situation.

Interest rates fell from a low point to the lowest level since records began and our savings started to dwindle as, to keep body and soul together in our retirement, and no longer able to rely on the interest we received, we had to start eating into them. We had to find ways to bolster our finances, or at least find a sticking plaster to stop the rot.

'We could let out the apartment in Spain for holidays, I suppose,' said Bee dubiously.
She had never liked the idea of letting anyone else use it and we had both agreed that we wanted to preserve it as our personal private piece of paradise.
I looked up from the depressing news feed on my iPad and said,
'No good, I'm afraid. The Foreign and Commonwealth

Office have just banned all travel abroad, so nobody from the UK will be able to get there, and I doubt if any Europeans will be allowed to go either.'

Many countries in the Eurozone were initially harder hit by the virus than the UK and, in Spain, even the Spanish were banned from visiting their own holiday homes, so we had no chance.

Dire warnings about the effects on the economy became the largest part of our daily news diet as things progressed and, as our eldest son was 'furloughed' by his employer and contemplated his huge mortgage with dismay, we realised we would have to hunker down for the long haul.

Boris Johnson, our Prime Minister, was upbeat, however. We had left the European Union, he reminded us, and when the 'Transition Period', which he refused to even contemplate extending, was over we could look forward to a "Brexit Bonus" and everything would be hunky-dory.

In the meantime, all we had to do was wash our hands a lot, and stay indoors.

Then he went down with the virus too.

-oo0Ooo-

I had enjoyed writing the 'Spain Tomorrow' series and, to my surprise, people were being very kind about it, and probably in search of a bit of escapism during lockdowns, started to buy the books in modest numbers.

It is well known that it is very difficult, if not impossible, to make much money out of publishing books. The income I received (at about 40p a book) had just about covered my advertising and promotion costs until this point, but now, as the 'royalty payments' and weekly sales numbers staggered erratically up from single figures to the heady heights of the dozens on occasions, it gave me an idea.

In a dusty cupboard, many years previously, I had disconsolately thrust away the manuscript of a 'thriller' I had haltingly worked on. Now, sneezing as I blew the dust off it, I pulled it out and read it through.

I had decided, when I first put it away, that it was in need of a bit of a re-write and now, looking at it again, I was certain. It was rubbish; so back in the cupboard it went.

Like the weather on the day I got it out, it was dull and dreary, and as a piece of writing it was 'trying too hard'. But getting it out had made me think.

People liked the lighthearted writing style of the Spain Tomorrow books, at least according to the now quite frequent reviews they were getting. So I wondered, could I write a lighthearted thriller? Was it even possible to combine humour with such a genre?

-ooo0oo-

Vitamin D, or rather the lack of it, was not helping me to deal with the repeated disappointments of my endlessly delayed and repeatedly cancelled cancer treatment, as the hospitals filled up with Covid-19 victims and all the staff were diverted to deal with the pandemic.

The virus took our neighbour and several people in our little town and I was told I could not go anywhere near a hospital (or even leave the house) until my case could be reviewed in early July.

Inevitably, by mid June, that review had also been cancelled 'until further notice', so I was beginning to feel that, if I didn't fill my time with something else, the strain might start to tell, and I would have to read that gloomy Government pamphlet about protecting my mental health after all.

Something had to be done.

So I started to do some research and made a few planning notes ... and then, as if by magic, 'The Menace Of Blood' fell from my pen.

All right, it wasn't really as easy as all that, it was actually a lot of work, but we needn't go into that.

It was short, certainly, but apparently, according to early readers, I had managed to inject pace and intrigue into the plot and it had a chance of capturing readers attention. The title may have hindered rather than helped because it was not about blood at all. It was actually about heredity and inheritance. But I found the easiest bit was writing in a lighthearted way; although the subject matter, particularly towards the climax as the characters cosy life was upended by a kidnapping, was anything but jolly.

I sent an early draft to a friend who had been very nice about my earlier scratchings and knew his way around proofreading, and made Bee read it again and again until her eyes bubbled.

I re-wrote it completely twice and then niggled away at some of the sections I was not happy with; but in what seemed like record time, it was done.

As the news got gloomier, I took the advice every writer must follow and laid it aside for a while, returning to another and more complicated (but still humorous) book I had started writing before. I thought for a moment about having another bash at the dust encrusted manuscript from years ago, but found the thought as depressing as the television news, so it stayed in the cupboard.

Pouring out 'The Menace Of Blood' had uncorked something however, and I found that work on the longer novel I was writing, entitled 'No Point Running', whilst not proceeding at quite such a blistering pace, was now coming along nicely.

I picked up 'The Menace Of Blood' again, re-wrote a couple of bits and found a few typos I had missed before. I got Bee to endure reading it one last time and then, taking a deep breath, I organised for it to be published.

Then, as I busied myself preparing marketing materials and advertisements for it, I waited.

-oo0Ooo-

In Spain, one of our neighbours, Wine Merchant Graham, was still struggling to get his angry red and snarly Ford Mustang car fixed and he complained that, despite the tight lockdown there, some people had taken up residence in the apartment above his.

Since the lockdown had been imposed, many people in the UK and in Spain had commented that things were so quiet that the birdsong in particular seemed more pronounced, and wildlife in general had become bolder and more visible.
It was not, as I worried, some animal in the apartment above Graham but, as he put it in one of his texts to me,
'I haven't seen them, but I can hear every scrape of a chair leg, slamming door, shower or pee they take!'
I was glad that our apartment, though nearby, is differently configured and has no neighbours above!

Clearly these people were breaking the lockdown and did not stay long, but a few weeks later Graham had further cause for complaint about his neighbours.

'Mustang liberated from mechanic and being driven by a friend at the moment,' his text started, but then, 'For the last three months we have had some gosh-awful neighbours behind us. Very noisy young drunks playing sh**ty music, and tonight a posse of very loud motorbikes ... This lot are Barcelona or Madrid pandemic escapees, I think,' and a few days later he complained of loud parties and 'nightclub music' all night from the same house.

This was really not at all typical of our little spot on the mountain, which was usually so peaceful, and while I confess that I breathed a sigh of relief that we were not actually there to witness this disturbance, it was another worry. I had read tales of undesirables breaking into empty property further down the coast on the Costa del Sol and squatting there, and I hoped the phenomenon had not migrated to our sleepy bit of the Costa Blanca. It was just one more thing for my worry pile.

Graham also reported that they had experienced another 'gota fria', one of the massive downpours which had caused so much flooding and devastation in previous years nearby, but that once again our mountain had effectively shed the water, to the dismay no doubt of those using the golf course below and on the coastal strip beyond, and for us at least no damage was done.

Meanwhile, back in the UK, in our home in rural Norfolk; Barkley, our 'almost corgi' rescue dog was barking happily. We were home all the time, which he seemed to take as a licence to bark freely whenever he felt like it, and although he only got one walk each day with Bee now, as I could no longer manage it, he enjoyed running about in the garden and harassing the birds.

Unfortunately our neighbours were of course also locked down and their frequent 'wheelie bin' shuffling, the noise of which always set barking-Barkley off, regularly interrupted the peace and birdsong we were now all so much more aware of.
To relieve the situation, Bee took him for ever longer walks and told of regular sitings of deer, various owls, rabbits, and kestrels when she returned from these walks through the adjacent fields. Even Barkley couldn't completely put all this wildlife off, it seemed, as she saw buzzards and even red kites on these walks. It was all rather nice.

In Spain, poor old Graham reported that the noisy young occupants of the villa on the road behind his apartment were actually legitimate tenants, renting from the absentee Spanish owner. At least they were not squatters, but something still had to be done.

Complaints were lodged. The security guards and resident's management association who are paid to protect the rather grand villas and 'executive homes' on our mountain, as well as (possibly as an afterthought) the handful of more humble dwellings like our apartment, in our little community were encouraged to act. And eventually, after some cajoling, they did.

At the same time Graham told me the sad news that his flawless 1957 Citroen had been sold to pay for the repairs to his mighty but temperamental Mustang. That meant our exciting plan to visit some of the better restaurants in the adjacent villages in style, in the iconic Citroen, was off, and that was disappointing.

Over the road, representatives were dispatched to confront the noisy tenants and the owner was contacted to deal with the matter. But instead of being apologetic, as you might expect, the owner was belligerent about the issue, and became defensive about his tenants rights!
Graham and I, discussing it over the internet, decided that these youngsters were probably his children or other family, sent to the relative safety of their coastal holiday home to wait out the virus and avoid the spread of contagion in the city.

The noise did eventually die down after this intervention, and in Spain, as in the UK, as the birdsong again became the prevalent sound (when Barkley wasn't barking), we breathed a collective sigh of relief.

-oo0Ooo-

As Boris told us, "We have left the EU" after all, another newsfeed announced that no unskilled workers from the EU were to be allowed in. A few weeks later it emerged that the Government's initiative to get English people to apply for jobs to help pick the crops to replace the European workers who had returned home, had failed. In addition, there were 122,000 unfilled care home worker vacancies which, for over six months, had attracted no English applicants.

We were warned we might be fined if we didn't wear facemarks in shops, now that the Government had dropped its assertion that they served no purpose. It was announced that we would not be joining the joint research and purchasing initiative the 27 countries of the EU had put their considerable weight behind and invited us to join, the purpose of which was to develop and produce a vaccine for Covid-19.

We would manage on our own, apparently, and if neither of our two vaccine trials bore fruit, we would compete with all the other countries in the world to buy any vaccine that might get developed abroad. This wasn't a triumph of dogma over common sense, Boris told us, because after all, we would have the 'Brexit Bonus' to fall back on and pay for all this, wouldn't we? That would make it all right.

The news was gloomy and the Government seemed to

be stumbling from one mistake to another, but you can't keep Bob and Bee down for long, and plucky to the last, we devised our own system to protect ourselves from Coronavirus and still travel to Spain safely without using aeroplanes or staying in hotels.

Now that the borders were opening and quarantine restrictions were gradually being withdrawn, and following the news that the 'shielding' regime was to be 'paused' from early August, we were free to move again. That was when we took the plunge and decided to buy that motorhome.

Simultaneously the postman bought news about my cancer treatment. That was finally going to re-start too, and there was a timetable for the weeks and weeks of daily treatments I would need to undergo at the local hospital.

Naturally we put our search for a motorhome on ice when we got this news. That plan changed almost immediately when an ideal one, with the all important and difficult-to-find automatic gearbox, as well as the sleeping and living arrangements we preferred, became available.

It was only a little over our absolute 'pip-squeaking, maximum clench' worst case budget, so we snapped it up and told ourselves that as soon as my treatment was completed we would be off to Spain in it, at last.

Of course it didn't work out like that and 2020 had more disappointments before it was done with us. But the motorhome budget issue was dismissed as small beer, when I realised that the daunting quotations I had had to get from private hospitals to treat me, when the NHS thought they could not do it in a timely manner, need not now be spent.

The motorhome was only a couple of years old, but cost about two-thirds of what we very nearly had to spend in private medical costs before, at long last, the NHS stepped up and offered me the lengthy diary of treatments in their letter.

It was too late for the 'spacer' they had fitted before the first lockdown, and that I had fought so hard and for so long to get them to recognise, fund, and install to protect my organs. That had a three month useful life before it would be useless and absorbed by the body, and as you can only have one of those installed, my treatment was not going to be without risk. However the Consultant said that time was now of the essence for my cancer, and I had to get on with it immediately.

The appointments in the letter were, I was assured, now fixed in tablets of stone, and could not be changed in any detail, come what may.

The first visit planned was for a series of scans (which I had had before, but due to all the delays and the expiration of the spacer, now needed doing again). Inevitably, almost before the ink was dry on that timetable, the hospital were on the phone pushing it all back several days. After that, though, the appointments were absolutely fixed, they said. Hmmm.

-oo0Ooo-

In Spain; after the estate managers visited the troublesome tenants, and following further discussions they had with the property owner, the noise stopped and matters calmed down on the mountain, as the usual peaceful lazy atmosphere was restored.

Not that we could experience it though. But at least Wine Merchant Graham was much relieved and his regular reports were much happier.

What also came out of the incident, however, was surprising.

Graham had gone round gathering up the contact details of most of our neighbours (be they Spanish, British, French, German or whatever) and got in touch with them all to urge them to support his efforts to get the estate managers to act. His plan worked, but more than that, we all started to communicate with each other by email.

Initially our correspondence was about the problem neighbours, of course, but ultimately the conversation turned to suggestions for meeting one another and doing what the British so rarely do, and getting to know our neighbours.

I enthusiastically supported this notion, although there was presently no chance of our going to Spain to take part. But as one of our newly befriended neighbours put it 'soon we can all meet up on one of our roof terraces in the warm sun with a glass of wine and enjoy each other's company.'
I wondered if such a thing would happen in the UK, but I was certainly looking forward to it!

-ooo0oo-

CHAPTER 4

Back home in sun starved and tapas free England, the strain of the lockdown was starting to show and it wasn't just because I was ill.

Our wheelie bin moving neighbour who wasn't going to work, had put one of his collection of cars up on blocks and acquired a metal wheeled trolley jack which, much to Barkley's annoyance, he pushed backwards and forwards down his paved path at the end of our garden several times a day.

This new sound drove Barkley crazy and despite our best efforts to distract him, his barking became even more frequent as a result.

As the weather improved and we spent much more time in the garden, we had to be ready to grab him and carry him back inside at a moments notice if the trolley jack or the wheelie bins set him off, and to quiet his barking with a distracting biscuit.

But it wasn't working. He was becoming increasingly

distressed by this and his reactive nature meant that, with more people around as we all had to stay at home, each sound caused him to leap up and, more often than not, give voice. Even when he was indoors.

We did what we could to calm him down, but on occasions we would find him lying panting and shaking on the tiled floor in our kitchen or conservatory, and I began to wonder if he was all right.

A trip to the vets had been planned, as it happened, because he was due to have his 'booster' injection. We were all dreading this and although on this occasion, because of 'shielding', I would not be allowed to accompany him, I worried if he would display the terror he had before at encountering the vet, and whether the whole exercise would be as fraught.

I was not wrong. It was awful, and while little Barkley did not lose control and pee on the vet's assistant's trousers this time, the vet was very worried about his stress levels and it was difficult for all concerned. Although pills to calm him down were dispensed, they seemed to have little effect.

Not long after the vet episode we got a letter from the Local Council warning us that there had been a complaint about dog barking and we were expected to do something about it.

The letter did not state which neighbour had complained of course, but we had our suspicions, and as the trolley jack and wheelie bins shuttled back and forth, and Barkley's signature vocalisations became ever worse, we realised something would have to be done.

I learned later that our neighbour was running a (probably illegal) commercial internet radio station from his summer house, at the bottom of his garden. Perhaps his microphone picked up Barkley barking on occasions through the thin wooden walls and that is why he became so annoyed about it.

We had engaged professional dog trainers who visited our home, in between lockdowns, to try to deal with the problem; attended classes, and bought all the training aids we could think of as we worked hard to mitigate the issue. But we had to admit that, while it had got a bit better than it was, Barkley still barked. A lot.

We got him from the Dog's Trust as a 'used dog' and we knew he had issues when we took him on.

We also knew he had been mistreated and was very 'reactive' ... but hey, we had trained two beautifully behaved labradors from puppies in the past, so how hard could it be to sort out little Barkley?

But it was hard, expensive and difficult; and while we did make a slight improvement over time, there was no getting away from the fact that this adorable little mutt was causing a problem still.

The Council sent a letter, the second we had received,

which warned that the situation was going to be monitored by the complainant (who they did not name, unlike the system in Spain where the recipient of a 'denuncia' could find out who was behind it). If necessary thereafter, the letter said, the Council may 'take action'.

We held a family meeting. We considered what options we had left and decided that we had pretty much exhausted all avenues.

I don't know if you are a dog lover, gentle reader, but I'm sure you understand that pets, and particularly one as beguiling as our nearly corgi, Barkley, become part of the family, and cannot be dismissed lightly or treated with detachment as, for example, farmers must treat livestock. But there was to be no getting away from it, the situation could not be allowed to continue.

I'd been told, when I received the cancer diagnosis, that while I waited for treatment I should avoid stressful situations and not dwell on matters. When Lockdown and Shielding were imposed that was increasingly difficult; particularly when, on the eve of it starting this time, my cancer treatment was cancelled yet again.

As I worried about the contents of the letter from the Council, I picked up and promptly put down the Government pamphlet about protecting my mental health. I must be strong, I told myself.

I confess I did have to choke back the tears during the

harrowing telephone call to the Dog's Trust, but they were very understanding, and as I haltingly set out the circumstances, it was agreed that they would take Barkley in, and endeavour to find him a new home.

I had made Barkley a promise when we adopted him and now it tore me to shreds to have to face the fact that I could not keep it. As Bee bravely drove him back to the Dog's Trust, I was inconsolable.

Because I was forced to maintain 'shielding' I could not even go with her, and I had to say goodbye to my little dog as he looked up at me trustingly from the sofa, and probably wondered why my eyes were leaking, and if I wanted a lick.

Writing this now might be cathartic. I hope so. I have been carrying about this burden of guilt and pain since that awful day, and as you might imagine, this has been very difficult for me to write.

Those around me said we had done the right thing and I do hope Barkley has found a new home where he will be loved and understood. I hated breaking my promise to him, and as I guiltily wrote out a cheque for the not insubstantial donation which accompanied the paperwork, in a futile attempt to ease my conscience, I knew it would take me a long time to get over this.

In between bouts of trolley jack and wheelie bin moving, when my neighbour dozes in the sun in his deckchair I hope he sleeps well, and when he broadcasts from his summerhouse on his internet radio channel hopefully he will now be undisturbed.

There is a post script to this story. We noticed, some weeks later, when we heard it barking, that he had acquired a dog of his own.

-ooo0oo-

CHAPTER 5

At last, following the arrival of yet another 'fixed' timetable, we were promised it was time for my radiotherapy treatment to start. Because of the Covid situation careful arrangements were made with the hospital to ensure that I only needed to spend the bare minimum of time each day inside their buildings.

I would be going to the hospital every day for several weeks, and with Coronavirus nowhere near under control, I admit I had concerns. But the cancer could wait no longer, it had to be done.

I made the following notes about my first visit which I hope will serve to quell the nerves of anyone facing a similar ordeal …

… *whilst I can think of better ways to spend a sunny morning, I have to say that actually it is not too bad. Apart from the self administered enema I have to inflict on my raddled body every day at home before we go, the actual procedure at the hospital is not as awful as it might have been.*

Of course the terrifying bit is actually going into the plague pit ... I mean hospital building, but we have developed a system with the consultants and staff to reduce the time I am there to the absolute minimum. As a severe asthmatic and therefore a sitting duck if this upper respiratory tract infection should get me, I am very grateful for that!

Today will be the first trial of this new arrival system, and I am the guinea pig.

On parking, windows wound up, in a specific disabled parking space as directed, I have to phone a special number and then, drinking the last of the 450 ml of water I must consume exactly ten minutes before the procedure, wait for them to call me back to say they are ready.

Then it is on with the new and unused face mask and into the building, trying not to touch anything.

I approach the transparent screens around the reception desk for a temperature check with one of those devices that doesn't actually touch me, I deal with a spoken questionnaire to establish if I, or anyone in my household has Covid symptoms and state my name and date of birth.

Having put the carpark ticket in the little scanner which is supposed to validate and mark it electronically, so that the machine by the barrier on the way out recognises that we are excused parking fees, I am then directed along a corridor to a specific waiting room.

As I get there, dreading having to sit and wait with other people, a voice behind me calls me by name and asks me to follow his rustling 'PPE' clad form straight into the 'suite' where the mighty zapper lurks.

Sometime is spent getting me, trouser-less, in the right position on the hard narrow metal bed in the darkened room, and the spacesuit clad nurses use green laser lines to locate and line up the tiny tattoos administered many months earlier before the latest spate of cancellations.

I can only see the eyes of the three masked medicos in the suite with me as they move around me and use marker pens here and there on my exposed flesh while talking quietly in numbers to each other, and they move me infinitesimally this way and that to line up the green light beams in the darkened room.

They offer me, now lying flat on my back, underpants removed with a piece of paper covering my embarrassment, what looks like, and almost certainly is, a rubber dog chew ring to hold with both hands so that I can keep my arms in the right position comfortably on the narrow bed with my hands clasped across my stomach.

Then, with entreaties to keep still, they leave the room, the bed moves backwards with a jerk and robotic arms, some with silver screens or panels and some without, move around me taking scans.

It goes quiet for a few minutes as I had been warned it would while presumably, unseen, they check my scans.

I've been on my own in the 'suite' now for a while trying

desperately to keep still and ignore the inevitable urges to scratch here or there, when at last two nurses appear and stick things on me in 'the affected areas' which will measure the radiation dose I am about to receive.

'Right,' says the chatty one, from behind her face mask, gently holding my arm in her gloved hand as I try not to tremble, 'We are ready. Here we go. Just wave your arm if you need us and please try to keep absolutely still.'

They leave the room again and, as the frightful machine starts to buzz and different robotic arms start moving in my peripheral vision, I am reminded of the effects of the earlier enema as the gargantuan device moves forward over me, and with a clank and a whirr gets into position.

A siren sounds. This is it!

It has gone quiet again. The machine has been, hopefully efficiently … no, make that 'no doubt efficiently' … moving about and buzzing loudly as it dispenses what they call 'a fraction' of radiation, and now it has folded itself up and returned to its original position.

With a jerk the bed moves forward and the nurses are here again.
'All done,' says the chatty one, 'any nausea?'

No, so I can get up, or rather down from the metal bed with the help of some steps. The decency covering paper is whipped away and I hastily re-don my underpants.

'This is your new treatment schedule,' she says, holding out a piece of paper, 'You will get one of these everyday *and it shows the time and which machine we will use. Shall I put it on this chair by your trousers?'*

I ask, and yes, I can put my trousers back on, and sanitiser is dispensed on my hands, as I notice behind me that the other nurse is sanitising every surface I have touched as well as the now sleeping machinery.

'See you tomorrow ... the exit is that way,' concludes the chatty one.

And that's it.

Back in the car and sloshing on the anti-bac lotion as advised. Even touching door handles and so on must be followed by this procedure.

The car park ticket doesn't work when we feed it into the machine by the barrier and we have the embarrassment of backing out, against the queue of traffic trying to escape from the hospital.

Bee puts on her mask and marches to the nearest doorway to ask what we should do.
It is the in-patient ward entrance where they take the Covid victims!

When she comes back I hand her an 'anti-bac wipe' and make her wipe everything, even the steering wheel, while she explains that the car park machine is faulty and she has to press a special button to alert unseen operatives to our plight who will make the barrier go up.

The car park machine only worked as it should

three times on our seemingly endless daily visits for treatment; and while we now knew how to deal with it and escape, without getting out of the car or approaching the wards again, it did rather add to the stress, as we hurried to get away from the hospital buildings each day.

Now it is all done, thank goodness, and whilst it would be many months before I could find out if it had worked, at least I could rejoin society (what there is left of it after the Covid ravages) and start to look forward again.

-ooO0oo-

In the week that Boris Johnson relaxed a lot of lockdown restrictions but said we were in for a difficult winter as the virus started to spike again, we grabbed the opportunity to travel … albeit just less than two hours from our Norfolk home, to get some fresh air.

It was threatening rain of course, but we were not downhearted. The motorhome didn't leak (so far) and was equipped with a cooker, fridge, shower and W.C., so we had all we needed and were completely self contained.
The couple of days of sun we did have even enabled us to have a barbecue beside our little travelling house, so we had nothing to complain about.

This time we chose a lovely spot on a small Caravan

Club approved camp site. It had a handful of bantam hens escaping regularly from their enclosure and the sounds of owls at night and buzzards amongst the myriad of bird life to watch in the daytime.

For company we had a little wren who popped about under our motorhome, appearing occasionally in the cut-outs in the wheel trims as he tried to catch the spiders, emerging hatchling crane flies and, if he was lucky, the smaller flies that were inevitably attracted to the windfalls in the adjacent fruit farm.

Bee managed to produce proper meals in the small, but remarkably well equipped motorhome 'galley' and as I wiped up the dishes after each meal, I slowly learned all the places she had designated to hide away all the essential kitchen equipment.

All very restful and helping my recovery from what the consultant warned was the equivalent of a major operation, delivered in dozens of individual parts over many weeks of daily visits to the hospital.

All too soon our short trip was over but I was convinced it had done me some good.

It's not Spain though, is it. That was still firmly off the agenda.

CHAPTER 6

Home again and I could concentrate on my avowed aim when all this started … to become a bestselling author. You may laugh, but progress had been made.

What defines a 'bestseller' depends on who you ask. Modern publishing methods, and the sheer number of books published each year make judgements difficult, but helpfully Amazon divide books into categories and using sales volumes through their site, I assume, can calculate which books sell best and therefore command the biggest audience.

The clever algorithms seem to do this live, with the numbers and therefore rankings changing constantly, but I was surprised when it was bought to my attention that 'Spain Tomorrow', my first book had entered the top 100 selling books in its category.
As these categories cover worldwide book sales with the largest book seller in the world this fact, astonishingly enough, meant it was officially a

'bestseller', and even more amazingly it stayed in the top 100 and even climbed higher in the next few weeks.

The competition is fierce, with between 600,000 and 800,000 books of all types published each year, so I was very excited to receive this information, as you might expect. I was also surprised, however, that my 'bestseller' was already in my hands.

So you might think, I must be raking in the royalties. Not so. The constant drain of marketing and advertising costs and the fact that there are so many fingers in the pie, as well as the Amazon Kindle and various publishing costs, means the money involved is not terribly substantial. But it is nice to get some beer money each month and I'm very grateful to everyone who buys my books.

Imagine my surprise, when I found out a few weeks later that 'Spain Tomorrow' had achieved the ranking of 5th most popular travel book; and then I was truly blown away to discover that it reached No. 3 in the rankings!

Now I really did have a bestseller, especially when it maintained that exalted position for several weeks and was eclipsed only by the hardy perennial 'The Travel Book' from Lonely Planet, which has sat in the number one slot for many years since it was first published.

For a very short spell my book even trumped the second placed tome, and then swapped positions around third to sixth place until, as I write this, it was once again clinging to a more modest place lower down the rankings for best travel book.

And the royalties? Surely from such a stellar position it must have increased my income ... not so. Not much happened as a result of this except Amazon offered me a one off payment to allow them to promote the book to Amazon Prime readers for 90 days, which of course I gleefully accepted. Thereafter things returned to normal and while I'm pleased to say that the sales continue at a steady pace, I will not be booking that world tour anytime soon!

-oo0Ooo-

In Spain, Wine Merchant Graham kindly volunteered to go and collect our car from the warehouse where we stored it near the airport, and return it to our own garage by our apartment.

Now that we had a motorhome and intended, when we were eventually allowed, to drive to Spain, we didn't need a car by the airport and whilst at that point we did not want to sell it, we were keen to save the storage costs.

All was not well with the car, however.
When Graham picked it up, apart from being filthy and in need of yet another new set of windscreen wipers, it had developed a fault and, after over a year in storage was not running well.

Graham, an incurable car enthusiast, stepped up, however.

Asking only that we cover the garage bills, he took it several times to his favoured motor mechanic, the proprietor of 'Mustang Sally' ... the workshop that also looked after his snarling Ford Mustang.

After much head scratching and a couple of false starts the problem was diagnosed and could begin to be sorted out.

During this time Graham also washed and polished it, vacuumed it out and treated it to fill ups with top quality fuel, all at his own expense, in an attempt to flush out the problem and cure the 'hesitation' it was suffering from.

Juan, the local mechanic, speaks not a word of English, and if we had to sort it out ourselves without Graham's contacts and resourcefulness we would have been in a frightful muddle, and stuck in the UK, would probably have had to send it to a main dealer and pay their extortionate rates to fix it.

Covid-19 stopped us going to Spain but Graham's generosity and kindness enabled us to address the problem at long distance and cement a firm friendship with our tremendous neighbour there.

All this had taken up a fair amount of Graham's time however, and I worried that we were imposing on him.

He explained that, with virtually no customers in the bars and restaurants due to the virus, business for wine merchants was vanishingly scarce, so he had the time to do this for us. He is a remarkably generous man.

As a final act he agreed to run the petrol in the tank right down to empty before taking it to Juan's workshop to be 'flushed out'. He found the process frustrating, however, and sent me a message headed 'Rotten little car!' in which he complained that, although he had used it to run many errands and undertaken a longish trip to visit friends some miles down the coast, it refused to drink much petrol and empty the tank!

Compared to his collection of cars, including the rumbling Mustang, his 'everyday' vast Mercedes and an elderly four wheel drive Jaguar with a big engine, a simple Ford Fiesta must be very frugal (Graham called it 'miserly') even if it is an automatic. At least our little car was getting something right!

-oo0Ooo-

It was still great having a holiday home in Spain even if we could not get there for the moment.

Friends there sent us regular pictures of the area around our lovely apartment, (which made me sad as well as happy) with details of what they were up to, to keep us connected.

Whilst stuck in rainy England I didn't usually have much to offer in return, but I was able to tell them about one little visit we made.

We went in our motor home to stay for a few nights in Suffolk, and while there decided to visit Southwold to find out what all the fuss was about.

Southwold is a quite attractive seaside town with a reputation for having eye-wateringly expensive, but much sought after beach huts, which can and do change hands for ridiculous amounts of money.
I believe the record is £120,000 but that may be out of date by now and I know that one was advertised for sale in 2018 for £150,000.

£120,000 for a shed? Crazy! We had to find out what the attraction was.

In the middle of the Covid crisis when we went, quite a bit of Southwold was shut, but the pier was still open and the management had installed a 'one way system' for pedestrians visiting to maintain 'social distancing'.

The area around the pier was quite busy with visitors of the older generation. Few were wearing masks and virtually all ignored the clearly marked one way walking route and shuffled along the pier however the fancy took them.

The Local Council had done their best, but clearly it wasn't anything these people thought need bother them, and they proceeded to the ice cream parlours and fish and chip restaurants as if times were normal.

We didn't stay long and were eager to get away from these thoughtless crowds, but we did find and examine the famed beach huts on the sea wall.

Whilst many were painted rainbow colours, they were nevertheless, just sheds. No toilets, no running water (unless you wanted to use a nearby communal stand pipe with one of those taps you have to push down and keep your hand on to make the water flow) and honestly not much going for them at all.

The candy stripes disguised rotting woodwork with salt spray clouded windows, and they had a general air of neglect.

The sheds ... sorry beach huts ... were arranged inches from their neighbours, on the slimy concrete sea defence wall; just far enough back, with the tide in, to avoid being splashed.
I noticed that they were each chained down to the bleak narrow concrete path and whilst they had a view from their slightly elevated position straight out to sea, the world and his wife could wander along the footway, so they had no privacy or private open space.

Only one was occupied when we passed by. A rotund gentleman was sitting in a beach chair with the double doors open and he filled almost all the available space. His wife, I assume, stood in the narrow gap beside him.

They wished us a cheery 'good morning' as the drizzle started again and, pleasantries exchanged, without even stopping for the obligatory 'take away' fish and chips, we scuttled back to the motorhome and retreated inland.

When you consider that even today £100,000 will buy you a perfectly serviceable holiday home in Spain with all modern conveniences, I just cannot see the attraction of buying a shed on a bleak sea wall in Suffolk, looking out at the chilly grey North Sea. But to each his own!

We returned to the camp site, where we were scheduled to stay, bemused.

-ooo0oo-

CHAPTER 7

Suddenly there were a couple of bright spots on the horizon.

The first, and most unexpected, occurred when my eldest son Richard and his delightful girlfriend Poppy came round for coffee one afternoon in late October. Not being allowed into the house due to the Coronavirus restrictions, we sat, socially distanced of course, bundled up in winter coats in the large carport beside our house.

Naturally enough the conversation was initially dominated by Richard's description of his recent hole-in-one at a local golf course. He was justifiably proud of this achievement and we made the right noises ... although, of course, whilst we had not seen him face to face since it had happened, we had heard the story before.

'Can't wait to show you how much I've improved if we get a chance to go to Spain and use the golf course there, Dad,' he added, but with the virus restrictions showing no sign of being eased, that was still some way off.

Richard and Poppy came bearing gifts. A box of biscuits (which Bee promptly announced she would put away for Christmas), a packet of my favourite shortbread fingers, some digestives and a bar of chocolate for Bee; all in one of those canvas 'bags for life' the supermarkets sell.

This bag was produced only when we all had our coffee and were joined by my youngest son, David.

Due to the need to maintain a two metre gap between us, Richard put it in the space between our garden chairs and retreated to his own seat at the other end of the carport. Bee unpacked the gifts with glee and we thanked them prettily for their kindness.

'Er ...' said Richard, 'Isn't there something else in there?'

This time Bee picked up the bag and looked; and then, with a gasp, drew out a white 'baby-grow' which was hidden in the bottom.
Richard and Poppy were going to have a baby!

This wonderful news was greeted with great joy and their subtle way of imparting it much praised.

The baby-grow was also printed with our surname under the word 'Baby' so there could be no mistaking what it meant, and Poppy said we were to keep it to remember this occasion by.

There wasn't a dry eye in the carport!

-oo0Ooo-

As so often happens in life, Poppy's wonderful news was almost immediately tempered days later, when her sister gave birth to a still born baby at eight months.
There are no words to describe that sort of grief.

-oo0Ooo-

The second piece of news concerned contact I had had from the hospital. It was arranged that I should visit our local doctor to have some tests and then, ten days later, stand by to receive a telephone call from the hospital Consultant at a set time and date.

It was time to find out if my cancer treatment had worked, and what the future held.

-oo0Ooo-

As the weather got steadily worse in England, and the rain in rural Norfolk became a more or less daily occurrence, a series of things needed attending to in the house.

The central heating pump, never the quietest of gadgets, ramped up its complaining whine to include a constant drumming and occasional shrieks, as more effort was demanded of it as the temperatures dropped.

Our 'tame' plumber who is charming and we have known for many years came and fitted a pricey, but mercifully quiet replacement, while we sat in the room furthest from the action with all the windows open and shouted pleasantries.

Then the conservatory sprung a leak. Well, two leaks actually.

First, one of the glass roof lights had an issue with a broken mechanism, but fortunately it could still be closed to repel the rain until replacement parts could be sourced. And then a damp patch appeared in a corner where water had obviously found its way in and run down the wall.

This conservatory was not very old and was still under warranty, but when we tried to call the company that installed it, all we got was an answering machine and although we left messages, no return of our calls.

-ooO0oo-

We took our motorhome out for a run on a briefly sunny mid-week morning to stop 'flat spots' developing on the tyres and to warm up the engine.

We drove to nearby Cromer, where there is a large carpark on the top of the cliffs by the sea, and we were surprised to find it busy with six or seven other motorhomes and camper vans amongst all the cars.

Staying overnight in this carpark is prohibited (the British Authorities take a dim view of any form of 'wild camping' pretty much anywhere and there are none of the prolific 'Aires' so treasured by motorhome owners in France and Spain) but most of these vehicles had occupants busily preparing cups of tea, or perhaps even a meal, while admiring the view.

We were delighted to join them, at a distance of course. Us in our 'van, them in theirs. And while we did not stay long, a few breaths of fresh sea air and the confidence our personal 'socially distanced' house on wheels provided was a great joy.

-ooO0oo-

CHAPTER 8

And along came Silke.

With all quiet on the travel front, another national lockdown threatened and ultimately imposed, something unexpected happened in my faltering career as a writer.

In Spain, Wine Merchant Graham had, you may recall, a delightful little black cat who lived with him in his apartment and went with him pretty much wherever he went, usually on a lead.

He discovered this comical little ball of fluff as a feral stray, being fed by a kindly property agent in an empty villa deserted by its foreign tenants.

After a long struggle and no doubt expensive vets bills, over many months Graham resolved this poor creature's health issues and trained her to walk on a lead and come when called. They were devoted to each other.

There was no doubt that this little cat had plenty of character and Graham took her all over Europe, including trips to England, on his travels. He also kept notes of her more hilarious escapades and diaries of their travels together.

It was Silke (pronounced Silk<u>EH</u>) who effected to introduce us to Graham in the previous summer, with her entreaties to be admired and fussed in the hallway near our apartment. Who could resist her sleek black fur, penetrating yellow eyes and her charming little chirrups and miaows?
Not Bob and Bee, and she soon found her way into our hearts.

That summer Graham was kind enough to tell us about his adventures with Silke and to show me some of his notes.
'I've often thought,' he said, as we sat sampling a new potential addition to his extensive wine merchant's catalogue, 'that it would be great to capture all these little stories in a book'.
And an idea was born.

'Silke The Cat, My Story' was published on 12th November 2020; having been written, for the most part, with Silke as 'narrator' from the notes Graham had made.

A seemingly endless stream of emails flew back and forth as I sat at my desk 'locked down and shielding' in rainy England. Meanwhile Graham was struggling to find buyers for his wines as the pandemic shut down tourism and the bars and restaurants he supplied in, still sunny, Spain. Creating the book provided us both with a useful distraction and lots of fun.

This joint effort was a completely new departure for me and the book was written to appeal to children as much as adults. We envisaged parents and grandparents showing children the numerous photographs taken by Graham throughout his association with Silke and reading them the humorous anecdotes and adventures. We also anticipated it would appeal to grown up cat lovers without children to entertain.

I was fortunate that Graham allowed me to give Silke a 'voice' in this book and we decided that the book would be narrated by Silke, as if she were speaking, with notes and editorial by Graham as we went along. I enjoyed juxtaposing Graham's descriptions of an incident with Silke's often differing view of the situation, and we both laughed at the jolly tales which emerged as we drew the book together.

Silke has her own Facebook page and I also wrote for that in 'Silke's voice' to amuse the growing following she was collecting as the book gathered pace. Those kindly followers were keen to express interest in the book when we announced what we were doing and we were grateful to them, and all the other cat lovers who discovered it, for providing us with an audience.

The book was launched as a paperback without a publisher (except me) just as the second national lockdown was imposed in England. This along with the approaching Christmas shopping round would, we hoped, help us to find readers. More people had time on their hands and the need to find a way to get a Christmas present to a friend or relative they were not able to see in person, so Amazon's mail order service fitted the bill perfectly.

During the long months it took to write this book, Graham and I considered producing it as an ebook, which we have now done so it is available for Kindle or e-readers.

Perhaps more adventurously we also discussed producing it as an 'Audio-book' (which is now available through Amazon's 'Audible' system) and even, as a follow up, a child's picture book or a Spanish translation.

If you think any of those ideas are worthy of consideration and the sort of thing you or your friends might buy, do please let me know.

Here is an extract of what you might expect to find in 'Silke The Cat, My Story' … now available from the Amazon bookstore as a paperback, an ebook and an audio book, using two charming young twin Spanish girls who are our neighbours in Spain to provide Silke's "voice". I hope you will forgive the blatant plug!

Meeting Bob and Bee
(an extract from Silke The Cat, My Story):-

… I may have mentioned that our new domicile has, in an outer hallway, stairs leading down to the underground garage where my human parks the car, but there are also steps going up.

My explorations on this higher level revealed nothing much of interest except a curious stout steel gate painted white.

I thought little of it until one day I perceived movement and, glancing up, saw that this gate was open and my keen cat senses told me that, during the night, humans had taken up occupation in whatever lay beyond it.

My cat senses are never wrong, as you would expect, and it was not long before my human noticed these people too.

I waited on the steps when they came out and gave a little chirrup to encourage them to admire me, if they were so minded. It is always my aim to be friendly to the neighbourhood humans and it often pays dividends in terms of treats.

These newcomers were no exception and soon succumbed to my charms, so I contrived to introduce them to my human.

People seem to like my human and he makes friends readily. It may be something to do with his being what I believe you humans call a 'wine merchant' and I have noticed that he regularly hands them bottles of that disgusting drink they all seem to like before they get happy and relaxed in his company.

The same pattern was followed by this new couple

from behind the metal gate and we were soon invited in to explore their home.

As is my policy, I looked under all the beds and into each of the rooms after a cursory inspection of the living areas. They seemed tidy enough, so I moved on to explore the wide terrace beyond some glass doors.

There was a table and chairs, as you might expect, and a fine view over the golf course far below, beyond the bridge where the ruffians live, to the sea beyond.

On my second visit the table was set with glasses and some plates and bowls, and once my human had deposited a large box full of bottles in the hall, we were invited to take a seat.

These people, who had introduced themselves as Bob and Bee, came from England it seemed, and I remembered the warm fluffy floors, rustling leaves and soft grass I had so enjoyed on our recent trips there.

As I was musing on these pleasant thoughts the man began to gently stroke me and I realised that, as we had England in common, we could become friends.

The female was fussing with something in the kitchen but then emerged with plates of treats including a selection of sliced meats.

I am normally very wary of this sort of thing as sometimes they are spicy and not to a cat's taste but, now on the man's knee, I could see that these meats may be worthy of further investigation.

The man took a morsel and quite politely offered me some, but my human warned him that I do not like spiced meats, so he should not be offended if I refused the sample.

However, one does not like to be impolite and having decided that this fellow and I could become friends, I leaned forward and took a little bite.

The flavour which filled my mouth was not at all what I expected. It was delightful, and I was soon back for more. In fact it was so good that, observing how I relished it, my human asked where he could buy some.

I found a soft red cushion on one of the leather sofas in the lounge, and when the breeze got up a little later, I made it my own. From here I could watch the happy humans on the terrace drinking and chatting amiably and I saw that my human had made firm friends with these newcomers.

A few days later, when I returned from a lively debate with the ruffians down by the bridge, my human grabbed me and put stinking stuff on the scratches I had sustained. It stung a lot, and I was very upset with him.

I was not in the mood therefore when, with much ceremony, he unwrapped some spiced ham which he said he had made a special trip to buy just for me.

Call me petulant if you like, but although I recognised it immediately as the same stuff the pleasant people behind the gate had offered me, after a disdainful sniff I strutted, with my nose in the air, onto the balcony.

Cats cannot be bought!

-ooO0oo-

CHAPTER 9

Another letter arrived signed by two MPs on behalf of the NHS.

It was to inform me that, now we were in 'lockdown' yet again, and as one of the exclusive 'Clinically Extremely Vulnerable' club who were at 'highest risk' from Covid-19, I had to start 'Shielding' all over again.

Not that they called it 'Shielding' this time. That word had too many connotations with stories of loneliness, mental health issues and isolation from last time. However, in six close-typed pages they laid out what I could, and could not do, and the stifling effect was much the same. Until it was reviewed in a month, I could not leave the house except for medical appointments and a bit of exercise in the garden. Nobody was allowed to visit me in my garden, and certainly not inside my house.

The rules about those who lived with me, Bee and David, my youngest son, were a bit more fluffy this time but, as I was waiting for the Hospital Consultant to pronounce on whether my recent cancer treatment had worked, it added one more thing to the worry pile. If I had not kept myself busy, this news would have allowed me time to think about my situation; which, as I was to find out, was not a good idea.

I was very grateful to be able to immerse myself in writing the 'Silke The Cat' book as well as adding to this chronicle. But when left to my own devices it quickly became clear that I was not as 'all right' as I thought I was.

This hit me hard when I was sitting in the car preparing to return home after a series of tests in the GP's surgery. These were designed to inform the hospital consultant of my progress ahead of the scheduled telephone consultation due in a few days.
As I sat fumbling with the keys, I found that I was crying.

The kindly nurse who dealt with the tests had made the fatal mistake of saying 'You have had such a tough year, never mind about Coronavirus, are you really feeling all right?'
I made positive noises, of course, but it was only when I got to the car that I allowed myself to dwell on what she had said, and if only to myself, I was able to answer the question honestly. Perhaps I was not quite as 'all right' as I pretended to be.

No matter, there was much to be done. The 'Silke' book had been proofread twice and Bee had read it once again just to be sure and given it her seal of approval, so it was time to publish.

But when it was done, and the weight of it was lifted from me, it was as though I was empty.

Graham, bless him, having never published anything before, had many questions for me to address and was bubbling over with ideas.

He kept me busy and occupied and, just as he had fixed my Spanish car, he started to fix me.

The conservatory got fixed too. The directors of the company who installed it finally responded to my increasingly panicky messages and, with half formed excuses about holidays and the difficulty of getting spare parts in the current crisis, turned up and resolved the issues.

As the weather was starting to get distinctly autumnal it was a relief, but the moment was tempered by the news from the MoT test garage that our English car needed four new tyres to pass the test.

They say these things come in threes ... I demand a re-count!

-ooo0oo-

We were back in lockdown again as Covid-19 deaths hit 50,000 in the UK, but on the eve of the restrictions coming into force, I was delighted to welcome Martin, 'The Top Notch Countryman' (as it said on the side of his van) once again to attend to the trees in our garden.

He was very well organised on matters of 'social distancing' and, when I offered refreshment and we agreed on coffee with two sugars, he produced a chipped cup which proclaimed he was the 'best Grandad in the world' which he positioned on a window cill beside the kitchen door.

'You make the coffee', he said, 'and pour it from your cup into this one so that nothing I've touched touches anything of yours and I'll be standing down there, by the trees, well away from you.'

The previous year he had asked if we would mind if he got a huge Harris Hawk on a show stand out of his van and put it on our patio where the bird could see him working, but not fly off. He explained that he had many birds of prey that he displayed at shows and he needed to get this young bird used to humans. This year he produced a magnificent Snowy Owl from his van, that he had raised from an abandoned egg.
'Gizmo', as the bird was called, was imprinted on him and entirely tame in his hands.

With another falconer he regularly took his collection of birds of prey to country shows and flew them to entertain the crowds. But he told me that he also provided a very interesting and unusual service for weddings.

This involved two trained birds with ribbons and a little pouch tied to their legs who flew into the church to the best man and groom to deliver the rings!

The participants were equipped with a leather glove for the bird to land on which they kept concealed until the last moment and then, no doubt to 'oohs and ahhs' from the unsuspecting congregation, they delivered their party piece.

Gizmo however, was no good for this job apparently, because he was so tame he would fly in as required, but then land on the ground near the wedding guests and waddle up to say hello in the hope of a friendly stroke!

I have mentioned the fascinating 'Top Notch Countryman' in 'More Spain Tomorrow' which preceded this book so I won't trouble you with another description, except to say that he is the most fascinating character and more than capable of expertly pruning our trees while chatting amiably about his exploits with wildlife. He is always a welcome sight on his annual visit to keep all our ornamental bushes, hedges and trees in fine fettle.

-ooO0oo-

CHAPTER 10

I had waited long enough and, whilst I admit I was nervous, I was also pleased that the time had come at last.

Almost exactly at the allotted hour the phone rang.

It was the Hospital Consultant, and she didn't waste time on preliminaries.

'I have the results of the recent tests here, and I'm calling to update you,' she said.

As a lifelong asthmatic, holding my breath has never been something I excelled at, but now I broke all records as I waited for her deliberations. Had the radiotherapy worked? Was the cancer gone?

'I'm afraid the nature of your cancer means it will be many years before I can give you a definite answer that it has actually gone, but I can say that based on these latest results it would appear that the radiotherapy MIGHT have worked; at least as far as we can tell at this stage.'

It wasn't a clean bill of health, and I knew from my reading around the subject that I could not expect that, but "MIGHT" was good, and I exhaled at last.

The plan now, I was informed, was to closely monitor the situation but allow my body to recover from the assault committed upon it a few months ago, and then test again.

The consultant reminded me that I had undergone the equivalent of a major operation, so it was bound to take some time for my body to heal itself, and particularly to recover from the collateral damage to adjacent organs, given that the hard fought for 'SpaceOAR' protection I had received many months before had dissolved away before the treatment even started, due to all the delays.

She added a little veneer of gloom by explaining that I would also have to deal with the effects of 'bronchiectasis' which is a lung condition related to my severe asthma and meant that I would still have to be very careful about infection, probably for life, and also that I could expect some further symptoms from the effects of radiation.

She would not go further than 'MIGHT' when it came to discussing the success of the various procedures, but she did set out a schedule for improving on that prognosis.

'In two years time,' she said 'after we have built up a good picture through testing and monitoring, we should be able to say whether the cancer has stopped growing.'

But she explained that it would be ten years before they could confidently state that it was beaten, and even that had a caveat in that she said 'probably beaten'.

Nevertheless this was all good news and my cancer journey was moving on. I was particularly delighted when she said that after a year of hot sweats, headaches, black depression and sudden attacks of absolute exhaustion among other, even less welcome, side effects, there was no need to continue with the hormone therapy I had been enduring, 'For now, though we can always re-start it if there is a problem,' she added.

It wasn't an unqualified green light, of course, but it did signify that I had pulled back from the precipice.

I had looked over the edge of that particular drop and whilst it was not something I ever wanted to do again, it had taught me to appreciate what I had and those around me, and to take a different view of how I used my time.

The thought that time can be finite can do that.

To celebrate we extracted the bottle of Prosecco which had been lurking in the fridge for many months, and having nothing to celebrate, had become something of a permanent fixture there. And we treated ourselves to a Mexican take-away to go with it.

The Mexican meal was awful, tasteless, overpriced, and cold, but nothing could dampen our mood.

I had started … oh all right, I 'MIGHT' have started to beat cancer!

-oo0Ooo-

I still had to observe 'Shielding' of course and the Government reminded me, in a series of letters, that I was still classed as 'Clinically Extremely Vulnerable', and the whole country was in 'Lockdown' once again as the Coronavirus pandemic raged around the world, but there was potentially good news on that as well.

The first company to declare results for a successful vaccine, Pfizer, claimed an almost 95% efficacy rate for its product and around the world efforts to prepare and manufacture it and other vaccines were also coming on stream.

The UK did not actually have a solid agreement to buy any of this particular vaccine, but our Government speculatively instigated official trials to see if our health service could approve it and declare it safe for use, in the hope that their overtures to the company would prove successful. Although at that point the company had decided only to apply for approval to licence their product in the USA and showed no inclination to involve any other Governments in assessing it.

In mid November, our Health Minister started to talk about rolling it out before Christmas for a few, and for the many in the New Year. None of the vaccine had been actually manufactured at that point, and it had no clinical approvals. The UK had not finalised a deal with Pfizer to supply anything yet. Nevertheless, it was the first glimmer of hope that our beleaguered nation had had since the previous March, and the politicians were clearly desperate to milk it for all it was worth.

Face was saved, to some extent, on the 23rd of November, when an Oxford University based joint venture with Astra Zeneca announced that they too had a vaccine that worked, and the politicians reminded us that they did have a relationship with that company, and had several million doses pre-ordered. There was still no official clinical approval for this new product, of course, and again none had actually been manufactured, but although it emerged that this vaccine had only a 70% efficacy rate at best, it was better than nothing.

The scientists behind it claimed its efficacy rate could rise to around 90% in certain circumstances, and although that was still some way behind the Pfizer product, at least we stood more of a chance of actually getting our hands on it, so the political community spread joy and anticipation throughout the land.

There was also a third declared successful vaccine at this point from a smaller manufacturer with whom the UK also had no business relationship. So news of that was quietly dropped as the spotlight turned onto the 'homegrown' product and we were assured that plans to give it official certification and the capability to manufacture it at pace, and in volume, were in hand.

On the second of December 2020, the UK Government's gamble paid off. The Pfizer-BioNTech vaccine was approved for use in the UK and plans to roll out the 800,000 doses we had ordered were made. There were many hurdles to deal with before it would be over, but as far as Covid-19 was concerned, the cavalry were coming over the hill at last. The supply chain was only just starting to gear up for production, but the UK was to be among the first countries to receive the vaccine!

-ooO0oo-

The Brexit situation, which had been rumbling on since 2016, was also coming to a head.

Seemingly endless deadlines came and went, as they had done with monotonous regularity since negotiations started. With no meaningful progress made, the real deadline, of January 2021 was looming large, and both the EU and the UK negotiators finally seemed to get a bit of a move on.

The three sticking points: trying to create a 'level playing field' for trade, the slippery issue of managing fisheries, and the rules for the 'Governance' of any agreement, remained the most difficult issues just as they had all those years ago when the UK started this torturous process. But at least the various Governments were focussing on these issues rather than dodging them now, and it seemed both sides accepted, at last, that securing a trade deal really was vital.

The run up to Christmas 2020 saw an intensification of activity on all sides as we sat, powerless to influence our fate, and in the hands of the squabbling politicians.

Attention turned to what this awful political exercise had cost, and even august Brexit supporting newspapers sheepishly published figures which revealed the costs to our economy of the Referendum in 2016. One newspaper even hysterically, and probably spuriously, predicted that the projected costs to finally get us out of the EU would probably come to even more than the amount we had actually paid into the EU, in the entirety of our forty odd years of membership.

Whether this bit of political dogma was worth it, in the face of the pandemic and the collapse of our economy is for history to decide. The question about whether it was really about our sovereignty or just raw political ambition also remains to be answered.

Against this backdrop, Boris Johnson promoted this own version of unreality when an independent investigation he had personally commissioned as to whether the Home Secretary was a bully, found that she was. But he said no, she wasn't, so she did not have to resign for breaking the ministerial code, but the hapless Civil Servant who penned the report had to resign instead.

This chaotic, and if it wasn't so serious, comical chapter of disasters unfolded as we wondered whether we dare lift the latest lockdown long enough for us to see our loved ones over Christmas and how many deaths would occur if we did.

All these uncertainties marked the close of 2020, a disastrous year that most of us would be very pleased to see the back of.

-ooo0oo-

In Spain, Wine Merchant Graham was preparing marketing plans and materials to help us sell 'Silke The Cat, My Story' as an ebook and a paperback to those who we hoped would buy it, to give as Christmas presents to cat loving grown-ups or to parents and grandparents to read the stories to the little ones.

Given that I was stuck in the UK and Graham and Silke were in Spain, he came up with an ingenious method for handling book signings, whereby he would have two rubber stamps of Silke's paw print made up, along with a copy of each of our signatures. He would then send me the one with his signature and Silke's paw print for UK signings, and retain the one depicting my signature to sit alongside Silke's mark when he attended book signings in Spain.

That plan didn't work when our preferred print shop owner declared it was too difficult to make a convincing rubber stamp of Silke's paw print, so we decided instead to have some stickers of the paw print produced to use at book signings. Now we just needed some book sales to make it all a reality.

-ooOOoo-

My smart new MacBook Pro was linked to a very old television, bequeathed to us by Bee's mother, affectionately known as Milly, who was responsible, although she didn't know it, for allowing us to buy most of our lovely apartment in Spain with the money she left us.

The telly may be old, but it had the all important HDMI socket and enabled me to write without squinting at a little screen without my glasses. This was progress, I thought.

'You could have dusted it off first,' said Bee, 'you mind you don't blow yourself up with that old thing!'

Thus chastened, I did clean it up and it has since enabled me to use the MacBook in comfort. This new laptop was bought to celebrate getting through my cancer treatment, and to serve as my Christmas, and at that price, my next three birthday presents, to myself. The TV was also one of the last of the generation of relatively small televisions so, unlike the vast shiny monster that very nearly covered one entire wall in David's bedroom (boys will be boys), it fits nicely on my desk.

Milly would have been impressed at my 're-purposing'. She was often loath to throw things away, as was typical of her generation. And I can imagine her looking over my shoulder, whilst peering uncomprehendingly at what was on the screen and saying,
'Very nice, dear. Can it pick up Radio Four?'

Christmas 2020 was going to be very different, with plans for a four day 'release' from lockdown to see family promptly shortened to one day only, Christmas Day itself, and then only for the minimum amount of time and, for most of us, only if it didn't involve travel. The discovery of first one, and then two, new and more virulent mutations of the virus shut everything down tight again. Although we stayed at home on our own, I can imagine worried conversations over the turkey and sprouts about whether the vaccines in development, and the one so far approved for use, were still effective against these new strains.

At lunchtime on Christmas Eve however, Boris Johnson was able to announce that a Brexit Trade Deal had at long last been reached with the EU, and for their part the EU announced that the UK had finally agreed to the terms of a trade deal, so that face was saved on both sides.

The EU's officials worked on Christmas Day to sell it to the Ambassadors of the 27 nations, and they approved it unanimously two days later. However Boris only released the full text of the agreement on Boxing Day and arranged for Parliament to discuss it the following Wednesday in order to keep the time allowed for Parliamentary and public scrutiny of the deal to an absolute minimum.

Christmas wishes were exchanged when Richard and Poppy pulled into our drive and stood by the door of their car while we had a shouted conversation from thirty feet away through the open lounge windows. It was nice to see them, but it didn't feel very festive.

-oo0Ooo-

On one side of the debate it was touted that those troublesome fishermen claimed they had been betrayed in the rush to get the deal done and that it was not in their best interests. But at last it came out into the open that the UK Government had come up with a plan to fund, in part at least, an expansion of the UK fishing fleet and its 'on shore' capabilities. They also acknowledged that we did not have the capacity to deal with an increase in the volume of fish unless we expanded the fleet. We could not have taken advantage of any increased catch we might have negotiated the right to claim straight away in any event.

Call me cynical if you like, but this sop to the big business corporations (controlled by certain politician's families among others) who own the UK fishing industry and stand to gain most from such a proposal, was probably the plan all along. The dispute about fishing, it seems to me, had nothing to do with 'sovereignty' or the hard pushed fishermen out on the high seas, and everything to do with commodity markets and vested interests.

Brexit however, as Boris triumphantly reminded us, was (mostly) done.
Just a few more 'T's' to cross and 'i's' to dot and it was over at last.
The sunlit uplands he had boasted about and the spurious claims on the side of the famous bus may be suppressed under a blizzard of bureaucracy and new form filling at the UK ports, as the lorry drivers trapped there over Christmas queued to have their Covid-19 tests before being allowed to leave the country for the Continent. But the Brexit clock had stopped ticking at last.

... Except in Gibraltar where the Spanish still had to agree the new arrangements with the Gibraltar Governor, of course.

Oh, and the Government still had to get the 'hard line' Brexiteers to vote for it in the UK Parliament, as well.

The Brexit clock had stopped and it was all over, they said ... bar the in-fighting!

-ooO0oo-

On Saturday 23rd of January 2021 I received my first dose of the Pfizer Covid vaccine and was told I had to wait until 17th April for my second dose, rather than the 21 days the manufacturer recommended, as the UK Government tried to issue as many first doses as possible and stretch out their limited supplies of the vaccine as far as they could.

History will decide if that was a wise policy, but I was delighted to receive my first dose, and although there was nothing definite as to when Bee could be vaccinated, somehow it seemed to bring the moment when we could at last return to Spain a little closer.

That was very good news as far as I was concerned.

In the following months Boris went, and so did his successor, and then her successor, and so it went on. I discovered that the TV had an 'off' button which made things very much quieter. It didn't solve the problems our battered and depressed nation had, but it helped keep them in perspective.

We had all been through a lot, and suffered greatly, but now it was time to rebuild.

-ooO0oo-

CHAPTER 11

Right, let's get up to date, and a bit more jolly!

I apologise to my readers if the previous pages struck a bit of a grim note, but it seems to me that some people I meet have wiped that awful time from their memories and now go on as if it didn't happen. It does us good to remind ourselves of how dreadful that period in our shared history was every now and again, so that we can count the blessings we have now.

My grandson is two years old as I write (in 2023) and he definitely counts as one of the very best of those blessings. Now the restrictions on gatherings are gone, Poppy and Richard, his adoring parents, are planning a wedding with all the trimmings and an extensive guest list. And from our point of view, at last we can travel freely again.

Much has happened in our lives too.

We have moved house to a 'wheelchair friendly' property with level access everywhere, a stair-lift and a bathroom with a big floor level shower designed to allow us to cope with increasing disability, if we have to face it.

It hasn't troubled us too much yet, thank goodness, but I had a bit of a wake up call when I started to suffer the symptoms of 'Pelvic Radiation Disease' (for which read radiation poisoning), along with a generous selection from the menu of possible 'later' side effects I had been warned about, following my cancer treatments. I won't bore you with a list, but suffice it to say they were not fun.

After a few trips within the UK in our motorhome, I had to admit that I was finding coping with it difficult and we were coming to the conclusion that this form of 'luxury camping' was not for us.

One of the main problems was that it was not easy to park such a big vehicle anywhere near the towns or attractions we wanted to visit, and as I cannot walk any distance, we were often frustrated when we toured in it. In addition, supermarket trips involved searching for two parking spaces, one behind the other, to get it in.

We tried attaching bicycles to the back of it but for some reason the manufacturer had decided to mount the rack to attach them high up, so that lifting the bikes, and especially my heavy electric bike was a real chore and not fair on Bee who, given my slowly disintegrating spine, had to take most of the strain.
We couldn't afford a 'Smart car' or motorcycles on

a trailer to tow behind it and looked enviously at those who had such contraptions on the campsites we visited.

For all that, it was actually quite easy and pleasant to drive, even if we did have to plan out routes carefully. But there was always the looming horror of emptying the cassette loo at the back of our minds, and let's be honest about it, nobody relishes that sort of job!

We could not believe our luck when, following an approach on a campsite from another camper, we were made an offer for it, which was quite a bit in excess of the price we had paid eighteen months earlier, so we decided to sell.

Our plan to drive it to Spain never came off, but we decided to drive our car there instead, staying in hotels along the way.

That turned out to be a great plan, and although the cheapish 'rep's special' hotels we stayed in beside the motorways were never going to earn great reviews, we only had to endure them for two or three nights until we were, at long last, back in Spain!

The imposition of the Schengen '90 days in 180' rules as a result of Brexit had effectively doubled our travelling expenses and stopped us being able to spend six months continually in Spain. But being able to spend three months there even if we had to spend the next three months in England before we were allowed to visit the EU again; and pay twice to travel, rather than staying put for six months at a time, was better than nothing, and we were eager to get over to Spain as soon as possible.

-oo0Ooo-

Of course our lovely apartment on the side of a mountain, overlooking the golf course and down to the Mediterranean sea beyond, was not quite as pristine as we had left it two and a half years before, and there was work to be done.

Our friend, neighbour and wine merchant, Graham had been keeping an eye on the place for us and held the keys. He also organised for it to be redecorated for us before we returned, and the decorator, an Englishman who worked for cash when not being an estate agent, had to deal with some damp patches which had developed whilst it was locked up.

Nevertheless, when we stumbled in exhausted after our long drive, I got to stand once more on my balcony enjoying the view.

There were occasions over the time we had to be away that I thought I might never see that view again and the relief to stand there, taking it all in, was quite overwhelming.

Bee, of course, called me a silly old what-not as I dried my eyes, but seeing that view again revitalised me and made me realise quite how good life is, and how lucky I have been.

I resolved then and there that we were going to have

fun and not let anything stand in our way as we re-familiarised ourselves with this wonderful corner of Spain.

Our first trip out was already planned.

-ooo0oo-

So, how are we doing on the 'bestseller' idea, you may ask.

At the point of writing I have written and published twelve books, and while none of them has been a runaway success like 'Spain Tomorrow' ...yet ... they are not doing too badly.

From that point of view the Covid lockdowns helped me and gave me something really positive to work on and learn about. My interest in writing has kept growing ever since.

'No Point Running', the hopefully amusing and engaging novel set in the 1970s, that I started writing during the first lockdown, is selling very well and reviewers have been kind enough to say it would make a good film!

The sequel to 'The Menace of Blood', entitled 'No Legacy of Blood' had some good reviews with calls for a further sequel to see what happened next.

And an entirely new series (which several people suggested would make a good TV serial) has been produced. This new venture starts with the mystery novel 'Double Life Insurance', which has a serious and involving plot, but is written in a lighthearted way.

In that book we first meet Bobbie Bassington, who has been the inspiration for several books so far.

'Bobbie and the Spanish Chap', is an amusing thriller about the adventures in Spain and the UK of this charming red-headed explosion as she graduates from Girton College, Cambridge.

Next we watch her grow and develop into a young trainee investigative journalist in 'Bobbie and the Crime-Fighting Auntie'. In that role she really starts something as she unravels an international fraud in 'Bobbie and the Wine Trouble' which again is set in the UK and Spain.
There is a thread of romance as well as tension in each of these stories and hopefully Bobbie will charm more readers as her stories become established.

Another thriller extending this series has just been published as I write this, 'Auntie Caroline's Last Case' draws all the strings together from the rest of the series and sees Bobbie solving her first murder. The subject matter may be serious, but the writing style is still lighthearted, and that I hope is the key.

If you will permit me just one more small plug, can I say that of course all my books are available as ebooks or paperbacks and can be found by entering 'Bob Able books' on the Amazon website search facility. What you will find there hopefully shows that I have been keeping busy! A proportion of the profits are also reserved for 'The Big C', Norfolk's cancer charity, who have helped me and who I would like to help in return.

I confess that when I started writing I had no idea how involving, complicated and time consuming the world of selling books is, let alone the time and work involved in actually writing them.

In a perfect world, publishers and literary agents would be quite a bit more approachable, and my first contractual arrangement with a publisher was not a happy experience. But we live and learn, and I hope my new arrangements will offer support and learning, rather than just milking money out of the process.

But that is not really the point. Doing something creative like this has been great therapy for me and when I was at my lowest ebb it perked me up and gave me a sense of purpose. I had never imagined it would be quite as all-consuming as it has become, but it is still enjoyable and no doubt helps to stimulate the little grey cells, which must count as good brain exercise!

I'm hoping for another best seller any day now!

-ooo0ooo-

There wasn't really anything specific to tell us something had gone wrong with the works. No oil on the floor or noises, and the first thing we noticed was that the air-conditioning was not blowing cold.

It took us a while to even notice that, in the middle of a bleak English winter, but soon enough we realised something must be wrong and an appointment was made to take our Volkswagen Golf into the local garage.

Re-gassing the air-conditioning was tried first, but only worked for a week, so back it went again.

'Ah. I was rather hoping this wouldn't happen,' said Mike, the charming Welsh proprietor of our favourite local garage who we entrusted with all our servicing needs. 'Pity, that.'

'Do you have to re-gas it again?' asked Bee.

'Well, no. Unfortunately this rather confirms our worst suspicions as to what is wrong with it, I'm afraid.'

Mike went on to explain that the gubbins which controls the air-conditioning on a Golf like ours is buried deep in the middle of the vehicle and quite inaccessible. When it fails it is a major undertaking to replace the failed components.

'Daft really,' explained Mike. 'I suppose they thought it was something that might not need any maintenance so they could get away with sticking it in the most awkward place. Volkswagen and Audi specialists dread this job.'

I was starting to dread it too, as Mike sent us away while he did his homework to establish if any new 'work-arounds' had been discovered since he last faced this problem, and to cost up all the components and the time the job would take.

'I'm proper embarrassed to have to tell you this,' he said on the phone a few days later. 'But even the, what shall we call them … less scrupulous end of the motor trade fight shy of this job. Even if we use 'pattern parts' it is still going to be expensive.'

Mike is not one of the more stereotypical motor engineers who look at big jobs as opportunities, or turn little jobs into big ones to inflate the price. Brought up 'strict chapel' in Wales and disarmingly straightforward, we had used him for years on the procession of cars which had passed through our hands and we knew he was not going to pull the wool over our eyes and would do his best to keep the cost down.

'So, I've had a bit of a think,' he said. 'You have been good customers to us and I'd like to think we have become friends over the years, so what I'm prepared to do is offer you a fixed labour price to try to put a cap on the job. I have looked into the main dealer's labour time for the job to work it out, but of course I won't be charging you their rates. In fact I think it will come in at about half what they would charge, once parts are taken into account. And we can get the full suite of parts delivered on a sale-or-return basis, so that when we get it apart, if some of the bits are serviceable we only need buy the broken bits.'

I swallowed hard.

'Why is this job so difficult?' I asked.

'The problem is you have to pretty much take the interior out of the car to get at the bits. The dashboard has to come out and that is a beast of a job in itself.'

'Oh dear. What is it going to cost, Mike?'

'I really am sorry about this, but if we have to use all the parts, it's going to be about £3,500.'

'Good God! How much?' I exclaimed.

'Yes, well,' said Mike, wincing slightly at my mild blasphemy, 'There might be a bit of a saving if we can return some of the parts, but honestly that is the best I can offer you, and obviously it's going to cost loads more than that at the main dealers. It is not going to be a quick job either. We think it might take about three full days.'

It actually took over a week and poor old Mike and the mechanics had to remove much more than the dashboard. When we passed by one day to see how they were getting on, we saw that the seats, the carpets and even the steering wheel had been removed.

'Horrible job this is,' said Mike, wiping his hands on a paper towel. 'I don't think we will want to do one of these again in the future, if we are offered. I know we are over the time we said to do it, but everybody we can spare has been on it, and as you can see it is still what you might call work in progress.'

Fortunately I had another car so we had transport, but Bee loved her Volkswagen Golf and we fretted at home waiting for Mike's call to say it was finished and how much the final bill would be.

Seven nail-biting days later we went to pick the car up. Mike, bless him, stuck to his price and although £3,500 was a lot of money to find, we knew he and his team had done their best and they can't have made much profit on the job.

'I've told the boys if someone else wants that job doing, on a Golf like, they are to say thanks, but no thanks. Horrible job that was. Never again.'

'When they strip a car down to that extent,' I told Bee on the short drive home, 'there is a danger things will rattle or not work so well. Perhaps we ought to sell it.'

'That might be true if we had taken it somewhere else,' Bee said. 'But Mike has always been good to us, and I think we should see how we get on driving it about normally for a while.'

'What about Spain?' I asked.

'We can decide if we are going to drive it to Spain nearer the time. Let's just see how we get on for now.'

I had no need to worry. Mike and his men had done an excellent job and the rattle free, ever reliable Golf took us to Spain and back without a hitch. And the air-conditioning performed faultlessly!

-oo0Ooo-

CHAPTER 12

T ime to move on.

In England, as 2022 opened a new world of possibilities before us, we decided to take stock of our situation.

We wanted to split our time between Spain and the UK as much as we could, but maintaining a house and garden in England was becoming a chore. I could not be much use in the garden any more and leaving all the work to Bee did not seem very fair.

Perhaps, we discussed, it was time to retire to somewhere like the New Forest, where we had spent our honeymoon and which we had always loved.

So we went for a look, and rapidly came away.

In darkest Norfolk we do get traffic of course, but nothing like the awful, seemingly endless, stop start queues we encountered there, both in and out of the tourist hotspots. And this wasn't even the school holidays!

Another rethink was called for.

I had a notion that it would be good to be able to walk to shops, cafes and restaurants and we thought a bungalow might be a practical idea. We started looking for property nearer to home in Norfolk.

'All these bungalows are tiny, and haven't been looked after. I'm certainly not living in a pig-pen like that last one we looked at! Some old people are so messy!' I announced.

'Well, we are trainee old people now,' Bee said. 'Maybe it is something we have to get used to.'

'There must be a better way than this,' I countered, and much to our surprise the solution was quite close at hand.

We called in Chris from the local estate agents. He was actually quite senior now, and usually would have sent one of his more junior staff out to our house, but we have known Chris for years and he has helped us with many property transactions, for family as well as us directly.

He came straight to the point.

'You will have noticed that the property market has gone completely mad in the last few months, with absolutely unheard of prices being achieved for very ordinary properties because there is so little on the market. Add the fact that, during the pandemic, demand built up but people were unable to move, and the whole thing is like a giant pressure cooker. The balloon is bound to burst eventually, of course, but there seems no sign of that happening yet.'

Chris told us the 'realistic' price we might expect to get for our house, but then added that, if we were serious about moving and had, for example found an empty property, he could present us with several "proceedable" or cash buyers who were likely to try to out-bid each other and fight it out to buy our house.

It was not a particularly special house. It was really just a modern developer box on an estate. In its favour, it was in a good position with one of the biggest and sunniest plots on the development, and was at the end of a private cul-de-sac. But that was all, really.

'We have known each other long enough for you to see that I'm not giving you the old estate agents snake oil here,' said Chris. 'The other agents will say the same. Mad prices are being achieved and buyers are fighting for every property.'

The seaside town of Cromer gets very busy in the summer season, but still has some vibrancy about it during the rest of the year. Unlike some seaside towns in England, it is very well kept and presents the visitor with every attraction, but without too much of a slant towards amusement arcades, and no riotous nightclubs. Like many of these places, it was once getting a little run-down, but the decay to the Victorian charm it offered had been stopped due to considerable investment and its ability to attract a better class of holiday maker.

On the outskirts but within walking distance, there are several quite up-market developments between the elegant villas well heeled Victorians built when the railway arrived. Some of their summer residences by the sea are converted to flats now, but several very substantial family houses still stand on tree lined avenues, and when they come up for sale they sell for quite strikingly high prices.

We had looked at a handful of scruffy bungalows in the surrounding villages and adjacent towns, but had no illusions that we could afford a bungalow within Cromer itself. We visited all the estate agents to see, of course, but came away empty handed.

We did find a very pleasant large detached bungalow on a corner plot in one of the less well thought of nearby towns. Although it was certainly not in a location we would have had at the top of our list in normal circumstances, it was at least available, and we got as far as expressing interest.

The owner said he was trying to buy an empty bungalow which had been the subject of lengthy probate negotiations, but now was ready to be sold. He wasn't being quite straight with us, however, and as time went on it emerged he was looking at other property and would not actually commit to buying anything.

He was what, Chris informed us, estate agents refer to a 'messer'. He had been messing about putting his bungalow on the market with various agents and taking it off again for a couple of years. In the end, when we got fed up and pulled out, the selling agent (not Chris this time) told him that they did not want to offer the property for sale anymore, thank you very much, because they had no confidence that he would ever actually commit to move.

Meanwhile, Chris was gently trying to persuade us to let him show a couple of people round our house.

'But we haven't found anything we can buy yet,' we said 'And we don't want to mess people about.'

'I'll be honest,' said Chris. 'A lot of people are putting their houses on the market to see what they can sell for and then pulling out if they can't find anything to buy. It might seem a bit underhand, but it does put them in a great position to buy something if they do manage to find a house they like. Nothing would move at all in this market if a few people didn't do that.'

I took his point. It seemed we would have to do the same to be able to compete for a property if we did find something to buy, or we were doomed to join the ranks of the "non-proceed-able" buyers and get nowhere.

Our youngest son who lived with us had decided that it was also time for him to take the plunge and buy a property of his own. Although he teased that we were throwing him out, he had been saving assiduously for several years, had ignored the temptations of youth, and single-mindedly scraped together a substantial deposit. As a single man, on a less than inspiring salary at the end of his apprenticeship with the local Ford dealership, the amount he could borrow as a mortgage was never going to be enough, so his only route into home ownership was to live frugally and save up cash. He had taken every overtime opportunity that came his way, did not drink, smoke or go to parties and was totally focused on just one all encompassing aim; to save enough to be able to buy a home of his own.

Living with us until he was twenty seven years old helped, no doubt. Both our sons also benefited from a gift towards their deposits from the bank of mum and dad, of course, but I was astonished to discover that he had saved up almost a third of the cost of the property he ultimately bought.

We were with him actually viewing the property he wanted to buy, with the car outside packed and ready, about to drive on our way down to Hampshire, when my phone rang.

Bee and I planned to go down to the New Forest for a couple of days for a 'serious look' for property, to decide if we did, or did not, want to move there, or if we were happier in much quieter Norfolk. We had given Chris, the Estate Agent, the key of our house to show people round while we were away.

Chris had arranged for seven "proceed-able" buyers to view our house and started to show them round, one after the other, almost before we had driven away.

Six of those viewers made offers. Five of those offers were quite a bit above the asking price, and one of them was tens of thousands above the price, and from a cash buyer.

Chris explained that this couple were living with their daughter and about to move to a rented house because they had sold up, but missed out twice on property they had wanted to buy. They were, Chris said, desperate to buy and thought our house was ideal.

Chris explained that they had lost considerable amounts of money during their abortive attempts to buy, and were now running up more costs with their furniture and effects in storage, and had 'unsatisfactory' living arrangements with family which needed to be resolved.

'Quite honestly, when they said what they were prepared to offer, we were quite taken aback,' said Chris. 'We knew their budget, of course, but when they offered all of it and said your house was just right, it was quite a surprise.'

'It's an enormous amount more than the asking price,' I spluttered. 'Do you think they are genuine?'

'I do. The last house they missed out on was through us, so we have done all the background checks and so on, and we know they have the money sitting in the bank ready.'

'But we haven't found anything to buy yet ...'

'No, but with an offer like that behind you, you are now in a very good position indeed to buy, and if you find something you like you should find negotiations somewhat easier.'

Blimey!

-oo0Ooo-

We viewed some lack-lustre property in and around the New Forest which helped us to decide that staying in Norfolk, the devil we knew as it were, would be better for us.

The one property which did impress us in Hampshire was what the agent referred to as a 'mansion flat'. A large country house split into apartments and 'wings' approached up a long drive with deer nibbling the grass in the grounds around it.

The apartment itself was in need of complete modernisation, dark, damp and draughty, but I loved the concept of a 'mansion flat' and it made me think a bit.

Before we came away we had visited the agents in Cromer again and gathered up such details as they had, and then cast them aside with barely a glance. Now home once more I picked them up, and preparing to condemn them to the recycling bin, one set of details did catch my eye.

It was a property in a badly photographed mews of quite attractive and obviously pleasant dwellings set around a courtyard. But what caught my attention was the address, which I recognised as the rather posh girls school my cousin had attended years ago.

As I read further I realised that the property in question was part of a twenty-five year old development on what I liked to imagine might have once been the school lacrosse or hockey fields, or something similar. And the grand old school building itself had been converted into luxury flats.

It emerged that this was to be an 'executors sale', so the property was empty and there was no 'chain' above it.

'Come and have a look at this, Bee,' I called.

'Well, it looks rather grand, I grant you, but the agent's blurb says it is a luxury apartment. It's what you called a "mansion flat".'

'Precisely,' I said. 'Shall I arrange a viewing?'

'Do we really want to live in a flat? There will be no garden.'

'A mansion flat,' I repeated, 'and they call them apartments when they are that posh. No garden to worry about when we are in Spain either, and if you look it has rather nice communal gardens that we can use but don't have to maintain. It's on the top floor, which is only one floor up, so it will be easy to 'lock up and leave' when we are abroad too. And it has entry-phones and all that sort of thing, so it will be quite secure.'

Bee took the agents details, and chewing her lip, read carefully.

'Hang on,' she said. 'This is an old peoples place, there is a stair-lift and level thresholds and all that sort of thing ...'

'Yes, all that must have been put in for the previous owner. It is an executors sale.'

'So someone died there?'

'Well, probably not actually there, but ...'

'It says the main bedroom is thirty feet long, and look at the sizes of the other rooms. It's enormous!'

'And in these rather better pictures,' I said, turning my laptop round, having found the details on-line, 'it has posh double doors from the dining room leading to the lounge, and two quite big bathrooms.'

'And a big kitchen breakfast room ... and a huge bay window ... and ceiling roses and a fireplace, and look at the size of that hall,' Bee noticed. 'Hang on though, that bathroom is bright pink!'

'And a thousand year lease with no age restrictions,

and a share of the freehold,' I added.

'But it's a flat,' said Bee. 'I thought we were looking for a detached bungalow?'

'It's an apartment or "mansion flat", if you prefer, and by the look of things, built in the grand victorian style and elegantly appointed with high ceilings. And it is in one of those posh roads in Cromer, near the cricket ground.'

'Richard played there a few times,' said Bee, recalling our eldest son's initially promising career as a cricket player when at school. 'It was nice round there.'

'Have you seen the price?' I asked.

So, after some more deliberation, we came to the conclusion that the all important 'location, location, location' trumped the fact that it wasn't a bungalow ... not that we could afford a bungalow in Cromer anyway, and we went for a look.

-oo0Ooo-

'The deer nibble the plants in the communal gardens' our prospective new neighbour, who we met by chance outside the apartment, told us as we chatted when we went for a look at the outside.

'That is a bit of a nuisance, but it is nice to see them, I suppose. They live in the woods at the end of the grounds and there is a path through to the sea and the golf course from there.'

'It is only a ten minute walk into the town, or fifteen minutes for you, dear,' said Bee.

'Thanks very much,' I said. 'I like the look of those coffee shops at the end of the road, and there is a really nice pub that does good food overlooking the sea a bit further on. Shall we go and give it a try?'

'I wondered when that idea would occur to you,' smiled Bee. 'Go on then!'

-oo0Ooo-

The sale and purchase proceeded with no more than the usual trauma, angst and stress as the lawyers performed with their habitual ineptitude and made a meal of the quite simple 'conveyancing' process.

That sort of thing always frustrates and annoys me. My career, before this writing thing grabbed me involved complicated multi-million pound property transactions, and I was responsible for instructing and managing a team of expensive high flying lawyers. I was accustomed to unravelling often quite complicated legal title and contractual issues. Simple domestic conveyancing really is ridiculously straight-forward in comparison to that sort of thing. And it never fails to amaze me how lawyers can make such a meal of it and make such obvious and self-evident omissions and miss-steps along the way. Jobs for the boys, I suppose, but the costs involved are not justified by the ease with which plain and simple 'registered title' can be transferred from one person to another in England.

The fly in the ointment, however, was the deceased vendor's daughter, who I christened 'Dolly Daydream'.

She and the other beneficiaries of the Will had met their designated solicitor in charge of the case, at the relevant office of the large multi branch lawyers practice, and tasks had been shared out amongst them. Perhaps, accepting her limitations, the group had given her just two tasks to perform.

Her first job was to arrange for the repair or replacement of the electric garage door which, somehow or other had become stuck almost, but not quite, shut. As a consequence we could not look in the garage before we bought the place and had to accept that the door would be fixed before completion took place.

It emerged that she lived part of the year in Spain, as it happened, but nowhere near our property, and was anxious to get back there. She also saw the inheritance she was due as her route to living in Spain full time, but money to achieve that was obviously tight, so she tried to arrange to fix the garage door 'on the cheap'.

As completion drew nearer, and her lawyer reminded her of her obligations to get it fixed, she engaged the services of a local 'expert' who gave her a quote to replace the existing burnt out mechanism with a new one. She clearly found the quote unpalatable and asked the 'expert' if there was a cheaper way.

Eventually, what he did was bodge it up with a scrap secondhand motor and gear from which he was going to scavenge parts before taking it to the dump. Dolly Daydream bought the machine at a knock down price, and the 'expert' connected it with a series of zip-ties (or cable ties), some insulating tape and a length of string. The mechanism was not a direct replacement for the broken one and the compromises made to make it fit resulted in an untidy, wobbly, and inevitably short lived, repair.

Dolly Daydream had fulfilled her obligations though, and as the 'expert' handed over the two scratched and dirty remote control fobs as he finished the job, she took the next flight back to Spain. With the fobs in her pocket.

The hiatus this caused when the lawyers could not hand over all the keys and we still could not get access to the garage on completion was, looking back, hilarious. Although it was not funny at the time.

Dolly Daydream seemed to have taken herself off for a holiday and left no contact details, so the lawyers could not immediately get hold of her to arrange to get the remote fobs sent back to England by courier. When they did eventually get hold of her she explained that she was in the process of moving house and had lost them.

Meanwhile the issue of her second little job appeared

on the horizon. She had not done anything about that either.

This second job was to arrange to clear the furniture and effects out of the apartment and have it cleaned.

At first, from Spain, she claimed she had not done it because she did not want the place to be unfurnished until after completion. As she saw it, if it was unfurnished, the property would not be presenting itself at its best, if it had to go back on the market.

The problem was compounded when our buyer, who was living in rented accommodation with his furniture in storage, if you recall, said he wanted to complete just a couple of days after exchange of contracts, or even on the same day if it could be arranged. We were fine with that and could completely understand his point of view so long as Dolly could finish her side of the bargain.

She had clearly not arranged for cleaners to go in and could not really do so until the furniture was cleared, but then she dug her heels in. No, she said, she would not get the furniture removed until after completion now.

She was back in England at this point and had apparently delivered the garage fobs, which she had subsequently found, to her solicitor. He used the opportunity to call a meeting with her and her brother, who lived near the property, to explain slowly and clearly to her that she could not leave the furniture in the property after completion and she had to get it removed beforehand.

At this point our buyer started to express his frustration at the delays. Who could blame him?

We were ready to go, with removal companies lined up and dates supposedly fixed, when Dolly announced that while she had arranged for an auction house to clear the furniture, she had forgotten to arrange for the cleaners. She was back in Spain again by then, so not in a position to do anything about it, she said.

Reluctantly I agreed that we would organise and pay for cleaners to go in ourselves, and my lawyer asked if the agents could give the keys to our cleaning contractor to get the job done.

No, said Dolly, when the agents asked. They were not to give the keys to anyone until completion had taken place and she had the money in her bank account.

Long distance, her solicitor metaphorically sat her down again and explained the problem she had created. But she dug her heels in once more and insisted that, at our expense, her lawyer was to draw up a legal agreement obligating us to collect and return the keys ourselves and to indemnify her against any damage our cleaner caused, while setting out that we had no right of occupation and could not hold the keys overnight.

Key-holder agreements like that are actually quite common, although Dolly's solicitor seemed to be quite out of her depth and floundered around trying to draw something up. Disappointingly, when I waded in to sort it out, our own lawyer was uncertain about this too, so in the end I produced a form of words which Dolly's lawyer basically accepted and knocked into shape for everyone to sign.

That all took three days and when the agreement was sent to Dolly to print, sign, scan and email back, it seemed there was a problem.

Dolly, it emerged had no access to a printer wherever it was she was staying in Spain, so after some head-scratching the lawyer arranged to get her brother to sign it and matters moved forward at last.

On the day of completion I arranged to visit the office of Dolly's lawyers in a nearby town about eight miles from the property, to pick up the garage remote key fobs. We were looking forward to finally seeing the inside of the garage we had just bought.

No, the lawyer's receptionist said, they did not have the keys logged as being on their premises, at all.

After further unnecessary panic, Dolly was contacted to ask what she had done with the keys, and it emerged that she had dropped them through the letterbox of the Cromer office of her lawyers, in an envelope, about half a mile from the property; not the branch that she and her brother actually used eight miles away, to save herself the journey to the office where her own lawyer worked. But she had not told either branch what she had done, or why.

After that was sorted out and the Cromer office discovered that yes, they did indeed have an envelope with some garage fobs in it, I picked them up there myself and joyfully returned to our new home to look inside our garage at last.

One week later the bodged and possibly dangerous electric closing mechanism failed and had to be removed. Our solicitor insisted that Dolly and her brother arranged for it to be taken away when I had disconnected it, and I confess to having one or two uncharitable thoughts about Dolly as a result.

Dolly's brother turned up to collect the scrap door mechanism after several reminders from the lawyer. But he turned up in a mini metro, which was much too small to accommodate the large and cumbersome garage gear. In the end, after some further delay, he sent a man with a van to collect it.

We now have a manually operated garage door rather than the electric one we paid for, and have to put up with it as it is.

Via the lawyers, during the sale process, Dolly filled in the lawyer's questionnaire, stating that the stairlift worked and had a service history. Needless to say it didn't work when you sat in the little chair, although with nobody aboard it could be made to travel up and down quite satisfactorily. Not quite fit for purpose then.

The instructions and papers left for us in the apartment showed that it had not been serviced for several years and that faults had been reported, but not fixed at that time.

I decided it was not worth getting into another battle with Dolly, my sanity was damaged quite enough, so we left it at that.

We had enough to think about tearing out that horrible pink bathroom, fitting a new kitchen and modernising the rest of the place. And I had promised Bee we would get all the work done before our next trip to Spain.

-ooo0oo-

CHAPTER 13

Wine merchant Graham used to live in Javea, a small town on the other side of the mountain range and very much an ex-pat enclave.

There is a picturesque but usually quite crowded man made beach in one part of the town and further along the coastal footpath, towards the little port, there are a series of restaurants and bars which serve an English breakfast. Sometimes the temptation is too strong and we travel to Javea with Graham and allow ourselves to indulge in this feast.

Our favourite place is 'Esquina' which, true to the meaning of its name is on a corner, right by a rocky section of the sea shore with a terrific view across the bay. English breakfast there costs under 12 euros and is served in a frying pan!

It may not be traditionally Spanish, but it certainly makes a pleasant occasional treat!

When we first bought our property in Spain I had

to buy and equip a barbecue. I made a series of mistakes with that which are documented in the first 'Spain Tomorrow' memoir. I bought charcoal when it was locally banned because of the fire hazard, and I was surprised to find what I thought were Aberdeen Angus beef burgers in a supermarket popular with Ex-Pats in Javea.

The meat, I later learned was actually 'Black Angus' not Aberdeen Angus and comes from the breed of beasts they use in bullfights, not their Scottish bovine cousins.

The point was picked up by a reviewer of course, who slightly misunderstood the difference as well, and criticised me for, as he saw it, selling out to the ExPat lifestyle by buying the cuts of meat we would recognise in the UK, rather than learning to shop like a local.

I doubt if you can get Aberdeen Angus on the Costa Blanca (although nothing would surprise me) and I have to say that the 'Black Angus', much prized by the locals, is especially delicious, and hey!... live and let live ... who cares if the ex-pats want to keep parts of their traditional lifestyle and their English breakfasts? As Boris probably wouldn't have said, 'we are all Europeans now.'

If, as we discovered locally, the Germans can have their bratwurst, the Italians their pasta and the Dutch their peculiar tobacco, why shouldn't the British enjoy the occasional greasy spoon breakfast?

Hang on though, in Esquina there was nothing greasy

about the breakfast they served. It was all freshly cooked, delightfully presented and not swimming in fat. The 'frying pan' it was served in was not really a cooking utensil, but a shaped plate. It was cooked, no doubt, on a 'plancha' and just served in this way to amuse the customers.

We are going to go back there again soon for another breakfast treat, I hope. And yes, it did feature on the list of the things I was looking forward to doing when we returned to Spain!

-ooo0oo-

Also on that list, and pretty near the top, was a visit to the little restaurant and bar at the bottom of 'our' mountain, run by the delightful Gabrielle and her multi lingual husband Miguel.

Usually, when we first arrive exhausted from travelling and to avoid having to cook or wash up, this delightful little spot is our first port of call. It also features on the last evening of our stays here for the same reason, and we regularly use it during our stay for a drink on a hot day or a lunchtime or evening meal, sometimes with friends.

It is situated next to an established tennis club which more recently also installed 'padel' facilities in glass sided courts. The regulars, from countries all around the world, collapse into chairs on the wide terrace outside the restaurant to recover from their exertions after games.

I suspect Bee would quite like a go at one or more of these energetic games, but she would not expect me to be able to join in. Watching from a safe distance behind the ball-stopping wire fences next door, at the tables close to the boundary, is as far as I go. But I do enjoy hearing the excited chatter, in several languages, of the players as they restore their tissues, often still in their sports kit, on the bars external terrace.

I am always terrifically impressed with the work of Miguel as he collects orders and passes the time of day with them each in their own language and fluently and seamlessly switches between languages, often holding conversations in three or four different languages at once!

The food there is also excellent, and considering that it sits on the edge of 'millionaires mountain' quite reasonably priced too.

-oo0Ooo-

Earlier, I mentioned that events had led to the suggestion that we should get together with our neighbours when the pandemic, and so forth, was over.

On our latest visit it actually happened, but rather than being a gregarious Spaniard who led the charge, it was our charming and unassuming Italian neighbours, Mario and Bianca who issued the invitations.

We are surrounded by folk from many nations in our home from home on the mountain but, as far as I know, only one set of Italians. Mario speaks a little Spanish and Bianca has a few English phrases, but communication with this delightful couple is not easy. We get by on smiles, gestures and attempts at phrases in common currency like 'OK' and 'Si'. The point is however that we do manage to exchange views quite adequately in this way, and when Mario threw his garden open for an extravaganza of food and wine for several of the neighbours we were delighted to be involved.

The idea was that each householder should make and bring along a typical dish which represented their home country.

Mario and Bianca provided a selection of home made pasta dishes of course, and a quite elaborate and utterly delicious sweet tart, which was Mario's personal speciality, of which he was justifiably proud. I was flattered that with his gentle touch on my arm he made it clear the he wanted me to be his assistant to hand round slices of this wonderful desert.

In what he described as his 'rumpus room', on the lower ground floor of his villa, he had set up a series of mis-matched tables, ranging from garden furniture to camping tables, which soon groaned under the weight of all the dishes carried in by neighbours. They came from Spain obviously, Germany, Holland, France, the

UK, and quite possibly other nations I have missed.

The eclectic mix of dishes was a real conversation starter as attempts were made to describe each dish in unfamiliar languages.

Bee pondered for some time about what she would prepare. Apart from fish and chips or an English breakfast, neither of which were practical dishes for such an occasion, especially when we might need to eat standing up, it was not easy to know what to present as typically British fare.

Graham the wine merchant had already nabbed the Shepherd's Pie slot, and presented a magnificent and very tasty dish with the potato topping attractively sculpted with a fork and crisped to perfection before serving. Graham, as a single man living on his own, loves eating, but had expressed concerns about actually cooking. He need have had no fear, his dish was delicious and much appreciated by all.

In the end Bee decided to prepare an unseasonal but at least British beef and ale stew, and we set about finding the ingredients.

The mushrooms were easy to come by and cans of Guinness served for the 'stout' she proposed to incorporate, but stewing steak was less easy to find, and nobody we asked had ever heard of cornflour for thickening.

Finally, and rather extravagantly, we ended up using diced filet steak for the meat, and considering about twenty portions were required, this was not going to be a cheap dish to prepare. It also took an age to cook and Bee, who had only really used the main oven to warm up croissants until this point, fretted about whether it was up to the job.

As with pretty much everything Bee cooks it was delicious of course, and with fresh parsley added to finish it off it looked a treat on the table in Mario's rumpus room surrounded by freshly baked bread and disposable plates and cutlery.

'Ah, goulash!' said one smiling German neighbour appreciatively. Well, not quite, but she did come back for a second helping!

Of course, as so often happens, it was only after the event that we thought of that other great British dish; apple crumble and custard; which would have fitted the bill perfectly and complemented Graham's shepherd's pie beautifully. Bee makes a mean apple crumble, but for now, instead, there are some 'sample' portions of the beef stew in our freezer. I was looking forward to those, and to the next of these gatherings. A consensus of those present said we should do it again and Bee will wheel out her apple crumble to many more appreciative comments then, no doubt.

Conversation at the event in Mario and Bianca's rumpus room was helped along by another of our neighbours who is Spanish but speaks excellent Italian, having attended a 'conservatory' there when honing her skills as a professional opera singer.

She came with her husband, who we learned is equally if not more accomplished, and in notes of performances we have seen, is referred to as "Maestro" as he wields his baton and conducts an orchestra. They perform together all over the world.

They brought along a quite spectacular homemade gazpacho and a tasty tortilla.

They chatted to everyone in that relaxed and unselfconscious way the Spanish seem to master so easily. They made smiling friendships with the likes of a German carpenter; a recently retired British Civil Servant; a couple of teachers from France; a Dutch used car salesman, a Spanish property manager; the English head of a catering school, and a host of other people, and acted as 'go-between' and interpreter in many conversations.

It all made for a wonderful and memorable afternoon.

-oo0Ooo-

CHAPTER 14

While this was going on, in our Spanish garden, Silke the cat took her ease, strategically positioned in a flower bed, ready to pounce on any passer-by of whom she did not approve.

She lives, as I may have mentioned, with Graham the wine merchant and is usually queen of all she surveys. But lately a new interloper had moved into one of the neighbouring properties, and as this was a puppy, Silke had concerns.

Further down the road another dog, 'Pinto' the diminutive but feisty miniature pinscher lives with his German humans. But Silke had quelled him and asserted her dominance over him many years ago. This new puppy, however, although still floppy and playful, was more of an unknown quantity.

'Grace', for that is the new dog's name is a sweet little cocker spaniel, and only a few months old. Silke, however is not easily charmed when an inquisitive nose is headed in her direction.

'Err, I'll grab the cat if you hold the dog,' said Graham.

'Our little dog will not be hurting your cat, surely?' asserted our Dutch neighbour.

'It is what the cat will do to the dog that worries me!' replied Graham, wrapping a snarling and spitting Silke in his embrace.

Silke was once feral and she certainly knows how to look after herself. Benign and even cuddly most of the time, when confronted with something that does not meet her exacting standards, she is quick to defend herself, perhaps believing that it is better to get your revenge in first!

When Graham and I wrote about Silke and her adventures in 'Silke the Cat, My Story' we did our best to explain, as far as we could, how Silke views the world. Most of it is gentle and sweet, but some of it has claws and teeth!

On that occasion Grace escaped with an earful of Silke's vitriol, but Graham made it clear to our neighbour that he might not always be on hand to step in, and recommended that the dog was attached to a lead.

For some time Graham had been working to restore the 'grass' which you have to cross to access our two properties.

It is not really grass at all, but some sort of ground

hugging shrub, maybe some sort of a conifer. It is planted profusely here to look like grass but submits to the mower, and is much more capable of dealing with drought and extreme heat. Since the automatic watering system we pay for with our community charges packed up, even this resilient plant has suffered and Graham has taken on the challenge of protecting it and even making it flourish in difficult circumstances.

Sometimes, at the very edge of this green sward, we might spot Elvis, a sleek black young male cat who perhaps has designs on Silke's territory. He might well look nervous though, as Silke has a series of concealed 'look-outs' in this area from which she can quickly mount an attack. We were quite worried the other day, however when Silke was first heard, and then seen in the gravelly part of the garden of an adjacent villa.

Silke was outnumbered. Elvis, twitching nervously, was joined by a tough looking tabby and a thin striped cat, and each took up positions in the corners of this area of garden.

Apparently fearlessly, Silke was setting out her terms for the strategic withdrawal of each of these interlopers, but as yet nobody was moving.

Silke tried again, a little louder this time.

The substantial tabby made his move. To Silke's annoyance he gave the ultimate snub and turned around so that his back was almost, though not quite, turned towards her and eyed her in an approximation of relaxed un-concern over his shoulder.

The skinny cat took this as a call to arms, and advanced, on her belly, a few inches towards Silke's defensive position.

It was too much, she had gone too far.

Silke released a low growl which rose by degrees, quite slowly, to a high pitched and very penetrating screech. If nothing else, it demonstrated the very considerable lung capacity of this quite compact cat.

The thin cat was convinced and backed a few feet towards a handy bush to give some cover. Not so the tabby who, to add insult to injury, stretched out a paw and yawned luxuriously.

As I called quietly to Bee to come and watch the unfolding drama, it all proved too much for Elvis, who bolted.

That, it transpired, was a wise strategy and triggered action when the tabby realised that without Elvis guarding his flank, his position was weakened.

There is a small low roofed brick built shed to one side of the drive close to the action, and a gate to the little road beyond it. This was how the tabby had come into the field of battle and in the blink of an eye he was up on the roof of this little structure and turning to see if he had been followed.

Silke stood her ground, or rather lowered herself into what appeared to any observer as a relaxed position with her paws under her body.

The thin striped cat realised that she was outflanked and on her own, and without further ado she turned and fled.

The big tabby lowered himself slowly from the little shed as Silke eyed him, and did his best impression of a nonchalant stroll for a few steps along the road, followed by a somewhat less cool dash for safety behind another property.

Silke looked left and right, and I'm sure she nodded in satisfaction, as she raised herself up and walked away. In her yellow eye as she caught mine, I got the distinct impression she was saying "Nothing to see here, human. Your assistance is not required. You may stand down!"

-oo0Ooo-

CHAPTER 15

Our decision to drive to Spain via the Channel Tunnel made our Spanish car rather surplus to requirements.

Graham had borrowed it on occasions and used it to run errands or just to keep everything moving throughout the pandemic period. The sensible Spanish system, whereby you insure the car rather than the individual drivers, meant there was no issue with him driving it. But we didn't need two cars in Spain when we were there, and we realised we could save the cost of the insurance as well as tax, and avoid the dreaded annual ITV test, the equivalent of the British MoT, if we sold it.

It would also mean we could put our English car in our garage so that we could save on the cost of car-washes when the inevitable 'Sahara rain' fell on it or it had to be parked under trees for birds to use for target practice.

It was handy to have a 'left-hand drive' car in Spain,

but certainly not essential.

'I'll buy it,' announced Graham, when we asked him about the procedure for selling a car in Spain. 'It is a good little car and would save me getting the Mustang or the Merc. out, just to run up to the shops and what-have-you, and it is much more economical to run than the Jag, which uses fuel faster than a petrol station.'

Well, that was a bit of a surprise.

That would make four cars for Graham, but he was serious.

He liked driving it around he said, and knew how we might be able to agree a price that would be fair and equitable to us both.

We looked together at the Spanish equivalent of 'Autotrader' on-line, and were both surprised at how much ordinary cars like our Ford Fiesta where fetching secondhand. Used cars in Spain are much more expensive than their equivalents in the UK and I asked Graham why that might be.

'It could be because the Spanish hang on to them longer and don't chop and change like the English, although I confess these prices are more than I expected.'

'Well, don't feel obliged,' I said. 'I wouldn't want you to feel that you had to buy it ...'

'Oh no,' said Graham. 'I said I want to buy it, and if

you will sell it to me for the prices we see here, I am happy to go ahead. I admit that the prices they fetch currently are more than I expected, but I have got quite used to the idea of owning that little car, and if that is what it is worth then that is what I'll pay.'

He would not be put off and when we found a very comparable car for sale on the website, he pointed at it and asked if I would take the price being asked for it.

It was a lot of money. I felt somewhat embarrassed, and I realised that it might not be such a good idea to sell a car to a friend. Supposing it went wrong? Friendship is more important than cars. But Graham was adamant. He wanted the car.

'And,' he said, 'I've been driving it about for months and months when you couldn't come here, so it's not as though I don't know what I'm getting. I've had the longest test drive in history!'

So we agreed and Graham organised the sale and the paperwork via that peculiar Spanish institution, a Gestor, and transferred the money to my Spanish bank.

Of course, a fortnight later, something went wrong with the electrics.

'Don't worry,' said Graham, 'I'll see what my tame mechanic thinks it is, but I should imagine it might just be a loose connection. Cars do go wrong, you know, no need to feel guilty. I always remember that Sir Gordon Borrie, I think it was, described a secondhand car as 'a collection of parts in varying stages of decay'. He was in charge of the Office of Fair Trade or something like that at the time...'

Graham knows what he is doing with cars and mercifully it was just a broken wire which was quickly fixed with a blob of solder, but I had visions of all sorts of problems and had nightmares that I had sold my friend a pup!

Bee and I bought Graham lunch when he would not let us pay for the repair, and thank goodness, the little Fiesta has been no trouble since!

-ooO0oo-

The money we got for the car helped towards the cost of modernising our new property in England.

Inflation was beginning to run riot and we decided that, while we were not able to secure the services of kitchen fitters with availability in their diaries before we left for Spain, we could at least get the kitchen units and appliances bought, and store them in the property to await our return, which would fix the prices.

We had 'interviewed' several kitchen fitters and been dismayed at how busy they all were, and the months we would have to wait to start the work. We learned that this was because of the Covid crisis and now that we were allowed, and had the confidence to get workmen in, everyone was spending money on their properties.

Our estate agent friend, Chris, frowned when he told us that, with property prices being quite so mad, many people had decided to stay-put and do up the houses they had. This further limited the supply of houses on the market and was making it increasingly difficult for him. He confirmed our suspicions that we had done well to move when we did.

The kitchen fitters we invited round to look at our job ranged from the 'avant-garde aspirational' to the 'jobsworth', and the elaborately over-priced to the too-cheap-to-be-true, and even included a chap who wanted to charge an hourly rate rather than give a fixed price for the whole job, but then would not commit to how long the work might take!

We asked several of the kitchen suppliers we visited to recommend fitters and at least three said we wanted Stu. He was the best they said, but pointed out that he was always booked up and we would be very lucky to get him this side of Christmas.

We collected his business card and got in touch with him. When he found out that, because of our planned trip to Spain, we did not need him until November, that the design was complete (I can design kitchens, fortunately) and the units would all be waiting for him on site, he asked if he could come and have a look at the job.

For a tradesman with such a glowing reputation

preceding him, Stu was modest, shy even, and concerned to get the details right.

He went away to work out a price with a copy of my plans and came back with a figure which was not the cheapest, but nowhere near the frankly ludicrous, most expensive quote we had, and agreed the dates we could book in his diary.

Just for once the delays created by our Spanish trip worked to our advantage. We had secured the most recommended kitchen fitter in the area. We might have to wait until we got back from Spain to fit it, but with Stu booked for the job we felt confident; so we ordered the kitchen and, swallowing hard, paid for it.

-ooO0oo-

Perhaps we were being just a bit too clever when we also appointed a bathroom fitter to turn the en-suite into a 'wet room' and replace the horrid pink suite in the second bathroom, at the same time as the kitchen work was going on.

The chap we engaged to do the bathrooms was the messiest workman I have ever encountered, and I've seen a few in a long career designing and building houses for work, and renovating others for my own occupation.

We had purchased all the equipment and sanitary

ware, and it sat in what was eventually going to be our main bedroom, next to the boxes containing the new kitchen. While Stu methodically organised the kitchen boxes into the order he would need them and stacked them tidily where we asked him to put them, the bathroom fitter simply unwrapped everything, threw away all the protective coverings (and the instructions) and proceeded to attack the first of the bathrooms with a hammer and bolster.

While Stu carefully applied sticky carpet and floor protection to every area where the workmen may step, the other 'team' set up a tile cutter in the hallway leading to the bedroom, and without thinking to cover up any furniture started blasting away with power-tools cutting off the old tiles.

When they had gone on the first day, Bee and I spent some time clearing up, and covering things up as best we could. In the morning we told the father and son bathroom team to at least close the door on their working area to confine the dust they were creating. Suitably contrite, they did do that, but had to be constantly reminded as the job progressed, and any venture into their working area involved crunching tile debris and dust underfoot into the carpets.

Stu, on the other hand, finished each day with a careful vacuum round and contained his working area as much as possible behind the kitchen door.

These sort of jobs are always organised chaos of course, and some mess was inevitable, but while

Stu started dead on time on the promised date, the bathroom fitter was a week late starting. Due, he said, to an 'overrun' on his previous job, and he was obviously trying to make up the time.

Time was an important consideration for us, too. Both contractors knew and agreed their programmes so that the work was finished well before we were due to leave for Spain again.

-ooO0oo-

At last it was over.
Stu, who it emerged is a time-served cabinet maker, not just a kitchen fitter, did a brilliant job and we are delighted with our new kitchen.

He made a shaped solid oak peninsular/breakfast table arrangement which was so heavy it took two to lift it into place, and that was after about a quarter of the timber had been cut away to make it the right shape. He spent a considerable time sculpting the curves on the breakfast table and then staining and polishing it until it glowed. It was, and is, a magnificent piece of work which draws admiring comments from all who see it.
As he finished up, to thank us for giving him the job, Stu made us an exquisite breadboard with sculpted in handles from some of this beautiful wood, which with its magnificent grain and colour, we were initially a little loath to use in case we spoilt it. It was good enough to frame and put on the wall!

The finishing work to the two bathrooms was not such a happy story, however. Granted, the younger of the bathroom fitting team did a good job of tiling, but his father was slapdash and obviously just wanted the job done and finished. Despite the fact that he was charging us nearly twice as much as Stu, because he had two men on the job whereas Stu worked alone, we had to watch him like a hawk to stop him cutting corners. We didn't catch every little cheat he employed until he had gone, however.

He used silicone bath sealant between the final patch of tiles because he couldn't be bothered to mix up any more grout, and we were glad to see the back of him. He had started a week late and also finished over a week late, so we were having to hold back other trades, like carpet and flooring fitters and so on; and he left the place in a mess.

One day, when finances allow and we can find a window in his diary, I am going to call Stu back in and ask him to make us a new folding door for a cupboard in one of the bathrooms which the bathroom fitters made an awful mess of. Instead of cutting a little from the top, and a little from the bottom so that the pressed pattern in the face of the door lined up with that on the adjacent one, he simply cut a large chunk off the bottom when I was not looking, hung it, and left it at that. It looks awful but we were forced to accept it because we had run out of time and we were anxious to bring the job to an end, and get this so called 'craftsman' out of our house!

Stu is welcome back anytime, however, and we were happy to recommend him to some friends and neighbours. I suspect his diary will always be full.

-oo0Ooo-

CHAPTER 16

We did finish all the work in time for our planned trip to Spain, and although we hadn't really had time to enjoy the finished renovation before we left, it gave us something to look forward to when we got back during the winter.

By then, we hoped, we would have got the hang of the whizzy new electric heating system we had installed, which replaced the wheezing, and no doubt downright dangerous, gas back-boiler system that was there when we moved in. Although Dolly Daydream stated on the lawyer's forms that it had been serviced, our own plumber was very dubious about that and said that he really ought to condemn it and shut it down, and that if he didn't know that we were about to rip it all out anyway, he would have done so.

It was very cold at the time, so we were eager to get it fixed.

Other than having the maximum amount of loft

insulation installed, and discovering an area where there was no insulation whatsoever in the vast attic, replacing the heating was the first job we did when we got the keys of the property. But the new expensive highly technical 'green' heating and hot water system we had installed to replace the gas boiler had complicated controls and we needed at least two lessons to learn how to 'drive' it!

Spain, when we got there was warm however, and we were very pleased to be back.

-ooO0oo-

'Let's go there for coffee,' said Bee.

The brand new and very attractive 'Fitness and Health Hotel' had recently opened and stood at the end of the mountain road that eventually leads to our apartment.

This stunning building was built to offer gym, training and recovery facilities to athletes and the many cyclists who use the roads in 'our' part of the Costa Blanca, as well as offering hotel accommodation to those who needed it. It has spectacular views down to the sea and a large swimming pool to one side with a sliding and folding curved roof to let in the sun.

We went up to the wide and stylishly furnished terrace, with a glass balcony making the best of the views, and strolled across the area of 'astro-turf' to get a better look.

I had been on this terrace before when I attended a free 'Coffee and Chat' session where people from many nations could meet and try to improve their Spanish in a relaxed and unpressurised informal way. The organisers told me that, so long as we each bought a coffee or a cold drink, the hotel made no charge for the use of the terrace or, in the unlikely event of inclement weather, the extensive lounge area inside, and looked upon it as one of their contributions to the life of the community. I had enthused about the setting when I got home after that session and Bee was keen to see it for herself.

There were extensive 'state of the art' and no doubt very expensive gym facilities in the wide glass fronted room below us, and as we walked into the building we could just make out the shapes of the exercise machines, and the people using them, through the smoked glass. These facilities were very popular it seemed.

The hotel was the dream of, and had been created by, a successful Russian cyclist and I read Bee part of their on-line brochure in which they describe what they are offering.

'It says on their website "...it is a full-service hotel and elite sport facility aimed at helping athletic teams and individuals improve their performance while training, rehabilitating, and recovering in a spectacular environment on the east coast of Spain.

"Our innovative training and clinic facilities are equipped with the latest technology and has a team of leading physiotherapists and trainers to assist with injury rehabilitation, nutrition, and a variety of therapeutic modalities. We offer hotel rooms equipped with hypoxic systems that simulate high altitudes for advanced training regimens." I've no idea what hypoxic systems are, but the coffee is good.

Surprisingly, after such a build up, the coffee was not expensive either.

"Alexander Kolobnev, with a long sporting career, having been an Olympic medalist in Beijing 2008 among many other achievements ..." I read on.

'Yes, well,' interrupted Bee. 'I grant you that it is a fantastic place, and I see they even have doctors and osteopaths and all sorts of things here, but as we only want a coffee, perhaps we are not quite ready for the full fitness make over.'

'By the look of all that heavy machinery in the gym, it would probably kill me!' I said.

'Come on then,' said Bee, as we paid for the coffee. 'Let's get out of here before I'm tempted to enquire about the cost of signing you up for one of their work-outs.'

-oo0Ooo-

Many of our favourite restaurants have gone, victims

of the prolonged shut down caused by Covid perhaps, but some survived, although perhaps in a different form, and we enjoyed reacquainting ourselves with them.

One of the first alterations we noticed was in the lovely indoor produce market in the nearby town where there are now seats, mostly bar stools, and tables for the customers beside all the little bars.

I have explained before how the delightful Marta, proprietor of one of these establishments, had fought long and hard for the right to provide a sitting area for customers at her premises. Now she had her wish, but perhaps in an unexpected way. The Covid rules about customers not standing at bars and so on have obviously led to a step change in how these places worked.

It was a delight to see that the market itself was still bustling and vibrant, with no shortage of splendid looking fresh produce to sell. In England there had been shortages of certain fruits and vegetables due, not to Covid, but to Brexit this time, but here in Spain the quantities for sale looked better and more abundant than ever.

The pandemic has caused many establishments to re-examine their priorities and the management of one of my favourite little outside bars, 'Gaudi' with its sprawling collection of outside seating in the Placa de Sant Antoni was now only open in the evenings.

All the chairs were still there during the day, but when

passers-by stopped and sat down, the waiters and waitresses of 'Ca Tona', the adjacent bar would dash out and redirect customers to their own seating next door. It amused us to note this territorial behaviour, particularly as one establishment's seats are almost touching those of the other in the sunny but crowded square, sharing the shade of the same palm trees. Perhaps the situation was reversed in the evenings, when Gaudi opened for business!

-ooOOoo-

So, what has changed since our last couple of visits to Spain?

Now that the Covid and Brexit horrors are receding, we can start to see what more permanent changes have been made, at least in our little corner of the Costa Blanca.

For a start there are considerably fewer Brits. Many scuttled back to the UK during the Brexit negotiations and although one or two are starting to come back, it seems many have given up and gone home permanently. We have noticed that there are (even) less menus and notices in English around, but there are more in Dutch and German.

According to the estate agents the Dutch particularly, are moving here and it is changing how the local businesses focus themselves now.

There are also quite a few more Germans, who find travelling here easy and have always regarded Spain as a good holiday destination. But the trend with the Dutch seems to be different, and they are not just here to buy holiday homes.

Several Germans, who are retirees I assume, seem to come and stay for six months over the winter, something we Brits are now unable to do after Brexit of course, but the Dutch seem to be moving in to live here full time.

That could be unique to our bit of the Costa Blanca, of course, but Netherlands number plates and accents are much more common than they used to be.

You know what Bob and Bee are like, we will cheerfully chat to anyone and try to make new friends wherever we go, and we have had several conversations with various charming new Dutch incomers in recent times.

The Dutch will probably get on well with the Spanish because, so my neighbour informs me, they are equally noisy. One of our new neighbours is particularly boisterous and likes to sit on his balcony in the sun with the television on in his lounge and the volume turned up so he can hear it outside. But, live and let live, is the Bob and Bee mantra, so we grin and bear it, and perhaps open another bottle of Cava.

I can say that all those we have met so far seem pleasant enough, although the Dutch are quite outspoken and direct. I have been told of instances where, if they don't like the colour you have painted your hall for example, they will tell you so, without any prompting, and go on to explain why the colour they painted their own hall is the correct choice.

As a personal example, I was told by one Dutch resident that I was being much too nice when discussing a minor point with one of our Estate Managers, and that I should be prepared to shout at him next time.

Not sure about that one, not quite my style.

Still, cultural differences are what it's all about, isn't it. We may only be a couple of part-time ex-pats, but we specifically set out to broaden our horizons and get to know and appreciate our European neighbours, and that is what we are trying to do. If we were all the same, how boring life would be, after all!

When we were first allowed to return, we noticed a lot of people were wearing masks and there was a nervousness about social distancing. This has reduced, and although we still do see people wearing masks, particularly from the older generations, it is now a rarity and the Spanish seem happy enough to consign social distancing to history.

Most of the Brits we meet appear to have forgotten about it altogether, and carry on as if the entire Covid thing never happened. The party atmosphere in some of the big towns an hour down the road from our little nest seems to be back, and the authorities are becoming concerned about crowds.

Let's hope we can keep Covid under control now

and that people around the world will not regret forgetting so easily about what happened and how bad it actually was.

Did somebody say another bottle of Cava?
¿Por qué no? (why not) as the Spanish would say!

-oo0Ooo-

The sea, of course is unchanging, but we did notice that the beaches nearby did not seem quite so crowded.

Not so in some Spanish towns. Some, such as Marbella, Benidorm and Barcelona who, having fretted for so long that Covid meant there were no tourists on whom they depended for their income, now complain that there were too many people about.

Their complaints were fuelled by fractious demonstrations by groups that declared tourism was destroying these places, but the initially factional activity soon became a trend, with Town Halls as well as individuals adding their voices.

I don't profess to know enough about this issue to feel able to comment, and they may well have a perfectly valid and reasonable case to make. But looking at the broader picture, beyond that particular bit of unrest, it does seem to me that we somehow need to have something to complain about to express ourselves nowadays, and to satisfy our human need to come together in groups, gangs or 'movements'.

Does there seem to be more of this since Covid stopped us meeting in common interest groups, or is it just me?

-ooOOoo-

On 'our' mountain, Silke the cat also feels the need to be sociable nowadays.

Silke enjoyed her summer, becoming a visiting cat for Wine Merchant Graham, rather than a house-cat. She made friends with absolutely everyone in the road and particularly seemed to like children aged between about 6 and 13, and she often followed mothers and daughters to their homes.

Silke has a little fat tummy which is emphasised by her unusually short back (I call her a 'short-wheelbase cat'). Many people had mistaken this tubbiness for pregnancy and Graham complained that some had glared at him for allowing an apparently pregnant cat to roam free.

'I could imagine several of them considering cat-napping her, thinking she was a stray, and taking her to a vet to be spayed yet again!' he said.

Silke, like many feral cats, has the top of one ear clipped to demonstrate to well meaning people that she has already been spayed, and cats so marked do not need scooping up and put through the procedure repeatedly. This clever solution is unfortunately not well publicised and vets are often presented with feral cats with one clipped ear, which they have to politely explain have been in before.

Graham, who lives in Spain full time, also told us that Silke spent a lot of time around one of our two pools, making many human friends. I was surprised to learn that she actually likes Elvis, the young and sleek black cat who lives down the road, and has formed an alliance with another neighbour's black cat who comes from the villas lower down the mountainside to visit.

But that is not to say she is everyone's friend. She has also been having stand offs with other cats at the end of the road and has been seen hiding under parked cars there when outnumbered or when the rain caught her out.

Graham told me she got caught several times in rain storms this year, although she seems to have associated rumbles of thunder with impending rain, and mostly makes it back inside before it starts. But sometimes she is too late. She really hates rain and Graham was much amused to catch her riding out a rainstorm on a neighbour's staircase rather than making the short dash for home recently.

'When it is not raining, her normal lair is on top of my BBQ on the balcony' Graham reports. 'But this year that was out of favour and right now her favourite place seems to be in the flowerbed under the hedge opposite your place, from where she can pounce on intruders or make a graceful appearance and charm those she favours, as the mood takes her.'

Silke was lucky to be rescued by such a doting human, and unless it is raining, makes friends with everyone she meets. She loves workmen, and one in particular who comes occasionally to maintain our property, and she inspects their work carefully, even climbing into their vans or sitting on their toolkits. Most of these visitors know her and refer to her as "la jefa", the boss!

-ooO0oo-

CHAPTER 17

'**P**asa Doble', or Latin American marching music associated with bull-fighting, greeted us at the little bar on the corner of two un-remarkable streets.

Apart from the fact that if you walked away from this bar, up the hill, you could see and would come to the ancient castle, this back-street location had little to commend it, but when we arrived there were no tables available and we had to wait by the open window style bar/servery to be seated.

It was hot, and getting hotter and Bee and I could use a cool drink.

'Shall we walk round the corner?' I asked. 'There are loads of bars and restaurants a little further down.'

'Hang on, that couple are going, I think,' said Bee, and she set off to grab the table while we had the chance.

It was the smell of sardines cooking that did it, of course. Just as appetising as bacon to a hungry traveller, 'sardinas a la plancha' soon has the customers salivating.

The waitress, or 'camerera' spoke no English, I doubt if she needed to in this place, but understood my order for "una tanque, una copa de vino blanco de la casa, y aqua sin gas, por favor," and with a smile produced a little pot with some shell-on prawns to keep us amused until the drinks came.

'Tanque', by the way, is a slang term for a very large beer, such as a pint served from a barrel. It means 'substantial' according to my dictionary. In typical Spanish style, the amount served is inconsistent and you might get a pint, or you might get less, but at the prices charged it is not really a concern.

The chalk boards, moving slightly in the merciful and very welcome breeze on this little corner, advertised a selection of 'tapa'. We ordered 'patatas bravas' and, of course the wonderful smelling 'sardinas' which were cooking somewhere within the little establishment.

I put a bit of top-spin on the words 'patatas bravas' and made the internationally recognised finger kissing gesture to emphasise my anticipation to the waitress. At that her face broke into a wide smile, and she said something which I did not catch, but which obviously indicated that she approved of and supported my choice; and what arrived was a large bowl of scaldingly hot roast potatoes covered in a finger-licking spicy sauce which more than lived up to expectations.

Star billing, of course, went to the 'sardinas'. Eight

good sized fish were served and we devoured them eagerly. They were delicious!

We had discovered another joyful Spanish place by stepping just a little away from the well tramped tourist routes and being prepared to attempt, however haltingly and unconvincingly, a bit of the local language.

As the tables gradually emptied, and we finished our little lunch, the chef/proprietor came out with a bowl of steaming mussels and sat down at a now empty table to eat them. He exchanged a few words with the remaining diners, most of whom he seemed to know, and gleefully attacked his lunch. If it was good enough for him, it was good enough for me, and I think I will order mussels next time we visit!

-oo0Ooo-

The name 'Limón Expres'(spelt the Spanish way) or 'Lemon Express' may have dropped out of popular usage over the years, but now this troubled but much loved little railway is running once again.

It is now officially called the Tranvía, and aspires to be a modern 'tram', but call it what you will this railway, originally built over a century ago to transport raisins and wine, the predominant exports of the region, has certainly moved with the times. It now moves people rather than produce.

Running between Denia and Benidorm where you

change for Alicante, the narrow gauge train passes through some of the most delightful scenery this part of Spain has to offer, and there is plenty to interest railway buffs too.

The route has to cope with some difficult challenges, particularly in the section between Altea and Denia and there are some very steep slopes, two and a half kilometres of tunnels, seventeen metal bridges over eight metres high, and seven viaducts.

Those familiar with the area will know that the terrain is mountainous and not at all ideal for railway building. Those mountains in its path a hundred years ago meant blasting out fourteen separate tunnels, one of which runs under almost all of the town of Altea.

By the mid 1970s the 'Lemon Express' was a popular tourist attraction much beloved of British tourists in particular. That period of its history started when a Brit invested in some old wooden 1920s railway carriages of the sort that had little outside balconies or decks at the back, reminiscent of wild-west movies. It was quite successful until the early 2000s when the line was becoming unreliable and in need of considerable investment, and the rolling stock was retired and the line closed.

Many tourists from that period remember with affection trips to the otherwise unexciting town of Gata de Gorgos to visit a guitar factory and some basket workshops, with a free glass of cava for the passengers on the way back!

When the line shut it became a political shuttlecock, and although fortunately the track was not actually torn up, it went through a period where proposals and plans for its development came and went, but little actually happened. But now at last, after considerable investment the line is open once again and we were keen to experience the scenic journey for ourselves.

The rolling stock is light years away from those wooden carriages, but, while not as romantic perhaps, at least the new part electric, part diesel 'tram style' carriages have air conditioning!

There was a bit of silliness to work around along the way however, which certainly made us smile.

The line from Alicante to Benidorm and then on to Teulada opened first but, because of the technical difficulties and the need to replace or reinforce the track between Teulada and Denia, that section of the route had to open a considerable time later.

When it was ready, however, new investment was made in more electric rolling stock for the last section, to make it as 'green' as possible. Unfortunately the trains they bought for the last section had different door heights to the rest, and the platforms, some of which had already been refurbished, had to be altered to accommodate the new trains!

There is now a bizarre sight to see, if you know it is there, and where to look. One platform surface is supported on props over another to raise it about half a metre to the correct height, and at the time we travelled it was necessary to change trains, not because the line went off in another direction, but because one type of train did not fit the platforms of the other part of the line!

By the time you read this they might have sorted it out, but when we first returned to Spain, eager to take our first ride on the new system, it did cause me to chuckle.

We can see the little train at the bottom of 'our' mountain, as it goes on its way to its final destination of Denia or, going the other way, off along the coast. Our mountain comes right down to the sea and prudently, all those years ago the railway builders decided to go round it, rather than to try to tunnel through it, so we can see the train in the distance on its broad curve as it passes by.

-ooOOoo-

The train, or tram if you prefer, stops in the pretty town of Altea, and we decided to visit.

There are actually two stations in Altea, and depending on what you want to see, you have to make sure you get off at the right one.

We, of course, got off at the wrong one. Not that there was anything wrong with the stop we got off at, and a short walk bought us to the sea and some bars. But what we wanted was the old town with its pretty, much photographed, flower bedecked streets, the handful of rather better restaurants, and the blue domed church we had heard so much about.

When we got back we told Graham, the Wine Merchant, what we had done and he immediately had a solution.

'There are a couple of really good restaurants there which I have been meaning to revisit for ages. How about I drive you over there one day, Bob, and deposit you both at the top end of the old town where I know you will find it a much easier walk?'

That was too good an opportunity to miss. We enjoy Graham's company very much, and his vast knowledge of the local eating places is something we often gratefully and gleefully make use of.

He doesn't really like being driven, and prefers to drive himself. So the chance to bring all these things together, and using his superior geographical knowledge to reduce the danger of me being not much use to anyone by the time we had walked to our destination, was something we were keen to do.

'I'll drop you just over there,' Graham said when the great day arrived. 'If you cross the road and toddle along that pedestrian street on the right it will open up into the main square. There is a slight hill, but from there you are only going up a bit. Hopefully after a couple of glasses of wine you will be feeling no pain on the way back, when you just need to walk downhill to the carpark!'

As good as his word, Graham dropped us in a most convenient spot and went to look for a space to park the car some way down the steep hill.

A mercifully short stroll up a fairly steep hill bought us to a lovely square, dominated on one side by the huge and very ornate church, and enclosed on the others by restaurants with pretty little roads leading down into the rest of the town.

Each of these narrow streets had dress shops (or perhaps I should say boutiques), and jewellery and trinket shops interspersed with bistros and bars. The traffic free roads all had steep broad steps so they would have presented me with something of a challenge if we were coming the other way.

Bee explored a few of the closer establishments while Graham installed me on the shady terrace of a bar with a beer, while he went to book a table at the almost adjacent restaurant which, he said, was his favourite in this part of the town.

He looked pleased when he returned a few moments later.

'The delightful Maite is still there and remembered me,' he announced. 'Normally all the good tables on the terrace are reserved, but she has got me that one you can see with the best view down to the sea, in about half an hour. Will that be long enough for Bee to explore, do you think?'

'You can ask her yourself,' I said. 'Here she comes now.'

The meal, whilst certainly not cheap, was frankly one of the most enjoyable we have had in Spain. Graham seemed to know all the staff, and the head waiter told us that the first of the new season's large white asparagus had just arrived that morning and he had some if we would like to try it. I love asparagus, but Bee hates it, so it does not appear on our menu at home. I grabbed my chance. It was delicious, of course.

We lingered over our meal, enjoying the view, each other's company, the gentle breeze and the glorious weather and, when it was time to leave, Graham explained where he had parked, some distance down the hill, and that he would go and bring the car up to meet us.

'No,' I said, invigorated by our excellent lunch and noting that the car was down, rather than up the hill. 'I am sure I can manage to walk down there, and you have been kind enough already by dropping us at the top.'

'Well, if you are sure ...' said Graham, as we paid the bill.

'After a meal like that I feel ready for anything!' I boasted.

The hill was very steep, but by taking it slowly, stick in hand, I managed the walk back to the car. I was glad when we got there however, because by this point it was getting very hot.

I felt fine, but somehow I felt as though something was missing.

As Bee started to climb into the back of the car I realised.

'Oh crikey,' I said. 'I've left my man-bag in the restaurant!'

This bag, I should point out, contains my glasses and medications so that, should the need arise, I have everything that I might want to hand. I discovered the joys and usefulness of a 'man-bag' when we first came to Spain and haven't been without one since.

Graham started to laugh, but the black look and stinging comments Bee was directing at me soon made it clear what would have to be done about this, and climbing up the hill we had just come down was considerably beyond me.

'Get in the car and put the air-con on so you don't fry, you twerp,' said Bee as she turned on her heel, squared her shoulders, and set off up the steep hill we had just come down to retrieve the missing bag.

Ever since then, whenever we go anywhere especially with Graham, I am constantly asked "have you got your bag" and am teased unmercifully about this unfortunate event.

I apologise if you have heard that story before, gentle reader. There can't be many left on the Costa Blanca that haven't heard it from one, or both, of my two companions by now!

CHAPTER 18

When all this started back in 2016, we first met Peter and Holly Gunn when they turned up to hand over the keys of a property we rented just down the mountain, while we negotiated to buy our apartment in Spain.

Coming full circle, we recently met Peter and Holly again at Marta's bar, now with seats, in the glorious market in Denia. This time we had planned to join them for a pizza later in a nearby restaurant which is their current favourite.

We have kept in touch over the years since we bought our lovely apartment and are most grateful to them for introducing us to solicitors and bank managers and helping us to get ready to deal with all the details of buying property in Spain.

Peter is one of those capable people who seems to know someone who can fix anything and he helped us to get our cooker fixed, which, with the useful diagnosis of 'He no get hot' from the Spanish engineer, took some time to sort out.

He even oversaw works to our property while we were in England when we had a security gate fitted, arranged to install better locks, and organised essential repairs to the sanitary ware in the bathroom. He introduced us to Kurt, the amazing and industrious air-conditioning installer, and sent his odd-job man, Denilo, round to get us out of scrapes on numerous occasions.

We also had a great time with them socially, eating out or attending the local 'fiesta', where they teased me after I made a fool of myself, dad-dancing on the closed off roadway which served for the evening as the impromptu dance floor.

We went with them to be introduced to the places they liked to eat, and discovered new places together to add to our favourites. We went to their glamorous villa, quite near our apartment, which had absolutely stunning uninterrupted sea views from the terrace by their swimming pool.

Their resourcefulness and kindness set us on a path to enjoy our corner of the Costa Blanca, and seeing them again brought back just how enjoyable our journey has been.

And now, joy of joys, flights from Norwich airstrip (it is little more than an airstrip really, although it is officially called an 'airport') to Alicante have resumed, albeit now under the banner of Ryanair so, barring the inevitable post Brexit difficulties with the Schengen

Rules, visas and so on, we will be able to travel to Spain easily once again.

And what of Brexit? Well, there is news on that. In the last few days as I write this, the Government have claimed a Brexit bonus victory for us, now that we are free of EU rules … wait for it … We can now produce wine in pint bottles!

"No one is going to make a pint-sized bottle," said one English winemaker, who asked not to be named, because the debate about imperial measures was so "toxic". "In order to make a pint-sized bottle you're going to have to invest a huge amount of money. It's a silly measure."

Here is what Kit Yates, writing in Byline Times had to say about the Brexit project to re-introduce Imperial measurements in January 2024.

"Rishi Sunak's Government has, over the Christmas break, quietly and unceremoniously dropped proposed plans to legislate for the large-scale increased use of the imperial system in the UK. It tried to hide the humiliating announcement behind a fanfare of publicity for a proposal to allow the sale of still and sparkling wine in pints – supposedly Churchill's favoured measure of champagne.

It's an embarrassing row-back on a project which began in earnest in the summer of 2022. Twenty months ago, Boris Johnson's Government shared a public consultation on one of the then Prime Minister's signature "Brexit Dividends" – the greater use of imperial weights and measures in the UK.

Upon hearing of the plans being dropped, Jacob Rees-Mogg, champion of the original survey, said "It is hard to see why this harmless little measure is not being implemented, especially as our largest trading partner, the United States, still uses imperial units."

Setting aside the fact that the EU is still by far the UK's largest trading partner, Rees-Mogg is also incorrect about the United States using imperial units.

Whilst it is true that the US remains one of only three countries worldwide not to make extensive use of a metric system, their US customary units are not the same as the UK's imperial measurements. An imperial pint is 1.2 pints in the US. A US gallon is approximately 0.83 imperial gallons. Either Rees-Mogg knew this and hoped that the rest of the country would buy his weak justification, or he didn't and was himself ignorant of the difference between the two anachronistic measurement systems."

What supreme stupidity we are capable of in Britain. I'm off to Spain!

Spain is a wonderful, fascinating, joyful and quirky place and we still love it just as much as we did on our first trip when we came 'just for a look, you understand' at property and ended up buying our much-loved apartment halfway up a mountain.

We hope, if you have the chance to experience Spain, you will adore it as much as we do, and that, if nothing else, the adventures, mistakes (lots of mistakes) and successes recorded in these chronicles will amuse you and help you to avoid making some of the bloomers we did.

Adiós amigos, hasta luego!

-ooO0oo-

ABOUT APAC

-ooOOoo-

Would you like to help the horses
(and dogs and goats) at APAC in Spain
mentioned earlier in this book?
Contact details and website address:-

APAC SPAIN

ABOUT THE AUTHOR

Bob Able is a bestselling writer of popular memoirs, fiction and thrillers. He describes himself as a 'part time ex-pat' splitting his time between his homes in coastal Spain and 'darkest Norfolk' in the UK.

His memoir **'Spain Tomorrow'** was rated as the third most popular travel book by Amazon in September 2020 and continues to top the charts. With the sequel **'More Spain Tomorrow'**, these charming lighthearted insights into his life continue to amuse readers.

His works of fiction such as **'No Point Running'**, **'Double Life Insurance'** and **'The Menace of Blood'** are also written in a lighthearted style, but combine pace and tension with fast moving engaging plots, and he has received many excellent reviews for his work.

All his books are available from the Amazon bookstore as ebooks and paperbacks and can be found by entering Bob Able in the search bar.

If you like Bob Able's distinctive writing style and would like to read more of his work, here is a little more information.....

Bob Able writes with a lighthearted touch and does not use graphic descriptions of sex or violence in his books, that is not his style. He prefers to leave that sort of thing to the reader's imagination.

He has also produced a new series of thrillers which will amuse as well as captivate riders. The Bobby Bassington Stories include:
'Bobbie And The Spanish Chap',
'Bobbie And The Crime-Fighting Auntie',
'Bobbie And The Wine Trouble'
And **'Auntie Caroline's Last Case'**

Bobbie makes her first appearance in the thriller **'Double Life Insurance',** and all these books can be read on their own, although if you read them as a series, **'Auntie Caroline's Last Case'** draws all the strings together and completes the tales of the lives of all the characters we met along the way.
Early reviewers had suggested that these stories would make an engaging TV series, and of course, Bob would be pleased to hear from television companies and promoters to explore that option!

His fictional novels include **'Double Life Insurance'** (where Bobbie Bassington first makes an appearance, fresh out of university), **'No Point Running'** (set in the world of horse racing in the 1970s), **'The Menace Of Blood'** (which is about inheritance, not gore) and the sequel **'No Legacy of Blood'**. They are fast-paced engaging thrillers, with a touch of romance and still with that gentle, signature

Bob Able humour.

His semi-fictional memoir **'Silke The Cat, My Story'**, written with his friend and wine merchant, Graham Austin and Silke the Cat herself, is completely different. Silke is a real cat, she lives today on the Costa Blanca, and her adventures, which she recounts in this amusing book, really happened (also available as an audio book).

The first book in the **'Spain Tomorrow'** series is a Bestseller. When it became the **third most popular travel book on Amazon** in late 2020, it was soon followed by its sequel, **'More Spain Tomorrow'**, and it continues to attract many good reviews and an appreciative audience in Europe, the United Kingdom, the USA and beyond.

Please leave a review on Amazon if you liked **'Third Helpings of Spain Tomorrow'** too.

STOP PRESS!!

Watch out for two new Bob Able books coming soon! **Sarah's Kitchen** *is a warm and cozy story and ideal as a 'beach read' and* **Blande and Trigg** *in a modern political satire in the form of a lighthearted novel.*

Contacts:

bobable693@gmail.com
This is a 'live email address' and is monitored by Bob himself, so do not expect automated replies ... Bob hates that sort of impersonal thing.

You can find details of how to buy all Bob's books and also follow him at:

www.amazon.co.uk/stores/Bob-Able/author/
B07VZBFFBZ

Or just enter **Bob Able books** on the Amazon site and the full list should appear.

He also has a website but, having the 'technical ability of a teaspoon', he hates updating it so don't expect too much!
www.bobable693.wixsite.com/spain-tomorrow

Disclaimer:

Copyright: Bob Able 2024

This memoir reflects the author's recollections of experiences over a period of time. In order to preserve the anonymity of the people he writes about, some names and locations have been changed. Certain individuals are composites, and dialogue and events have been created from memory, and in some cases, compressed to facilitate a natural narrative.

Thank you for reading. You may like to know that Bob Able contributes to 'The Big C', Norfolk's Cancer Charity, who have helped Bob with his own cancer battle and who do great practical work to help cancer victims and promote research. Find out more at: www.big-c.co.uk

*An extract from '**No Point Running**',
Bob Able's thriller set in the 1970s:-*

'Well, life was simpler in 1978, I suppose you
could say. No mobile phones or internet or any
of that rot, and Amazon was still just a river.
Mind you, that didn't stop me, as a former car
thief and telephone sanitiser getting involved,
as a guest at a country house with the horse
racing set, and almost getting murdered,
amongst the highest levels of society; twice.'

Chapter 1

On Tuesday, at 17:15, I died.

No doubt the swarm of nurses, doctors and sundry hangers-on checked all the pipes, wires and tubes and, when the heart monitor confirmed my status, they were galvanised into action. After some unseemly pummelling and the injection of stimulants, at 17:32, according to the notes on the clipboard at the end of my bed, I breathed again. It had been close, but for some, not close enough.

Allow me to explain.

I'm not actually a bad lad but I have, how shall we say, found the straight and narrow path a little constraining at times. My employment, such as it was, for the last couple of years had mostly involved motor cars, and their removal. But not just any cars, I only procured high end stuff, to order, and for immediate shipment abroad.

The owners of the luxurious or sometimes fast and flashy vehicles hadn't actually handed me the keys and sent me on my way with a cheery wave, so some upset was to be expected if I was disturbed in my work.

Josh Pindar was a case in point. He had made his money bookmaking and his Bentley Continental, with his pretentious JSP 123 number plate, was testament to his success. But when I took it for a spin and accidentally sold it, he became quite cross and decided to seek me out.

There were to be no police searches for Josh though. He didn't want any flatfooted bluebottles eyeing up his operation, so he decided on a different strategy.

He put the word out that he was looking for a replacement for the Bentley, by fair means or foul, and at the earliest possible date. To that end Big Mel, one of his associates, picked up on the request and contacted Tinker Pete who it just so happened occasionally commissioned my services.

Of course it wasn't Tinker Pete I was working for when I nicked Josh's first Bentley and he had no idea of the connection. It was just bad luck that Tinker Pete was the person Big Mel approached with quite an exacting brief as to the colour and specification required and Tinker Pete engaged me to fulfil the order.

I'd arranged to meet Big Mel in a bar by Wimbledon station at a certain date and time and innocently enough explained that, if I could find one, actually pinching the motor would be no problem as I had made a comparable acquisition just a week ago for one of my overseas clients.

I thought Big Mel's reaction was a little unusual in that his eyes widened and a muscle in his ample jaw twitched when I dropped this pearl of wisdom, but I thought nothing of it at the time.

Big Mel bought me another drink and asked me to study the specification of the car his boss required and I, foolishly I now realise, expressed my surprise that it was the absolute spit of the one I had recently lifted.
'Popular choice, it seems. 'I added as Mel excused himself to make a call from the phone box outside.

I remember him coming back to the table, and that nerve in his jaw jumping, but that was it until I woke up in the hospital bed.

Having counted my limbs, felt my teeth with my tongue and tried, painfully, to move my arms and legs, I established that I was somewhat bruised, but broadly still in one piece. My head, however, had gained a solid attachment to an unseen jackhammer and I decided, then and there, that a change of career might be an attractive proposition.

I was good at what I did, however, and had never troubled the police with my activities so I was somewhat surprised to find, as focus returned and I could make out more of my surroundings, that a uniformed female police officer was standing by my bed.

The significance of her presence became clearer when she said, 'Ah, he's coming round, 'and to me, 'have you any idea how this happened to you?'

A nurse, who I had not noticed until this point, hustled her aside and said something along the lines that this was not the time for questions, and would she please wait in the hall.

As my faculties began to return, I noticed that this efficient

nurse was strikingly pretty. She was bustling about checking the monitors and so forth when she said,
'So how are you feeling?'
Somewhat painfully a kernel of a thought was trying to make its presence known in my aching head.

In my profession, if you can call it that, it is unwise to carry any form of identification on the person and, as the meeting with Big Mel did not involve using my tools, they remained at home when I met him.
Could it be, I wondered....

I tried a tentative 'Where am I? 'and the nurse, who had her rather shapely back to me at the time, turned around.

'Now you just try to relax, 'she was saying, 'what's your name by the way?'

The idea that had been tapping on my cerebral cortex demanding attention burst into life in my head.

'My, my name? 'I mumbled, 'I, what .... Oh my head!'

I added a couple of groans for good measure and left it at that, there being no apparent need to rush these things.

But things were moving fast anyway, and here was a white coated individual, complete with stethoscope and clip board who had questions of his own for me.

All in all, these interludes helped with my ideas for a change of career. Could acting be my destiny, or perhaps selling life insurance? It certainly seemed the nurse, the doctor and now the lady police officer were eating up my little show and were hungry for more.

Eventually they explained to me that I was scraped up from behind the bins at the back of the bar in Wimbledon and deposited here by persons unknown who had the use of the company ambulance.
The chef, or similar, at the bar had discovered me as he collected his bicycle at the end of the lunchtime shift, and called the

authorities.

As I gathered this information I expressed surprise at every turn and, hopefully without over doing it, continued to deny all knowledge of my address, reason for splattering the bins with a good deal of my vital claret, or for that matter giving my name.

Various doctors came and went, including one in a suit who asked me all sorts of leading questions and was, I suspect, sent to see if I was making up the memory loss thing.
I was careful and, jackhammer allowing, thoughtful in my responses and it seems I got away with it.

You can find details of how to buy 'No Point Running' and all Bob's books at:

www.amazon.co.uk/stores/Bob-Able/author

Printed in Great Britain
by Amazon